CHILDREN'S GUIDE TO SANTA FE

CHILDREN'S GUIDE TO SANTA FE

Anne Hillerman

SUNSTONE PRESS
SANTA FE

© 2005 by Anne Hillerman. All rights reserved.

No part of this book may be reproduced in any form or by any electronic or mechanical means including information storage and retrieval systems without permission in writing from the publisher,
except by a reviewer who may quote brief passages in a review.

Sunstone books may be purchased for educational, business, or sales promotional use. For information please write: Special Markets Department, Sunstone Press, P.O. Box 2321, Santa Fe, New Mexico 87504-2321.

Library of Congress Cataloging-in-Publication Data:

Hillerman, Anne, 1949-
 Children's guide to Santa Fe / by Anne Hillerman.— Rev. ed.
    p. cm.
 ISBN 0-86534-448-5 (softcover : alk. paper)
 1. Family recreation—New Mexico—Santa Fe—Guidebooks. 2. Santa Fe (N.M.)—Guidebooks. I. Title.

F804.S23H55 2005
917.89'560454—dc22

2005026324

WWW.SUNSTONEPRESS.COM
SUNSTONE PRESS / POST OFFICE BOX 2321 / SANTA FE, NM 87504-2321 /USA
(505) 988-4418 / *ORDERS ONLY* (800) 243-5644 / FAX (505) 988-1025

To Mom and Dad

who taught me to appreciate Santa Fe—and much, much more—
when I was a girl growing up in Santa Fe.

And with appreciation to everyone who helped me get the
information together and the book finished.

Contents

INTRODUCTION FOR PARENTS AND OTHER GROWNUPS / 11
INTRODUCTION FOR CHILDREN / 14
FACTS ABOUT NEW MEXICO / 15
WANT TO LEARN MORE? / 16
A TOUCH OF HISTORY / 18
SANTA FE TIMELINE / 24

PLACES TO VISIT / 28
    Santa Fe Children's Museum / 30
    Santa Fe Farmers Market / 32
    Georgia O'Keeffe Museum / 34
    Institute of American Indian Arts Museum / 36
    Libraries / 37
    Museum of Fine Arts / 39
    Museum of Indian Arts & Culture/Laboratory of Anthropology / 40
    Museum of International Folk Art / 42
    Museum of Spanish Colonial Art / 44
    Palace of the Governors / 46
    Palace of the Governors Portal / 47
    The Planetarium / 49
    El Rancho de las Golondrinas / 50
    Shidoni Foundry, Inc. / 52
    Wheelwright Museum of the American Indian / 53

ARTS AND CULTURE / 54
    Arts Alive on Milner Plaza! / 56
    Aspen Santa Fe Ballet / 57
    Fine Arts for Children & Teens (FACT) / 58
    GirlsFilmSchool / 60
    Institute for Spanish Arts / 61
    The Lensic Performing Arts Center / 62
    Los Alamos Concert Association / 63
    The National Dance Institute of New Mexico / 64
    O'Keeffe Art and Leadership Programs / 66
    Santa Fe Chamber Music Festival / 67
    Santa Fe Community Orchestra / 69

Santa Fe New Music / 70
Santa Fe Opera / 72
Santa Fe Performing Arts School & Company / 74
Santa Fe Pro Musica / 76
Santa Fe Symphony / 78
The Santa Fe Youth Symphony / 79
Site Santa Fe / 80
Southwest Children's Theater Productions / 81
Warehouse 21 / 83

GET MOVIN' / 84

Fishing / 87
Hike and Bike / 89
Horseback Riding / 94
Public Parks and Playgrounds / 95
Randall Davey Audubon / 104
River Rafting / 105
Winter Sports / 107

KIDS' CLUBS AND PROGRAMS / 113

Big Brothers Big Sisters of Santa Fe / 114
Boy Scouts of America / 115
Girl Incorporated of Santa Fe / 116
Girl Scouts Sangre de Cristo Council / 118
Kids Stuff and Kids Camps / 120
Monica Roybal Center / 121
Santa Fe Boys & Girls Clubs / 122
Santa Fe County 4-H / 123
Special Olympics of New Mexico Area 2 / 125
Sports and Organized Recreation / 126

DAY TRIPS / 128

Albuquerque / 130
    The Albuquerque Aquarium / 130
    The Albuquerque Museum of Art & History / 132
    Explora! / 133
    The Indian Pueblo Cultural Center / 134
    National Hispanic Cultural Center / 135
    The Lodestar Astronomy Center / 137
    New Mexico Museum of Natural History and Science / 138
    Rio Grande Botanic Garden / 140
    Rio Grande Zoo / 142
    Sandia Peak Tramway / 144

    Los Alamos / 146
        Los Alamos Historical Museum / 147
        Bradbury Science Museum / 147
        Los Alamos Demonstration Garden / 149
        Valles Caldera National Preserve / 149
        Bandelier National Monument / 150
    Elsewhere / 152
        Kasha-Katuwe Tent Rocks and Cochiti Lake / 152-153
        Pecos National Historic Park / 154
        Pueblo Indian Villages Near Santa Fe / 156
        Santa Fe Southern Railroad / 161
        Wildlife West Nature Park / 162

SPECIAL EVENTS FOR KIDS AND FAMILIES / 163
    Santa Fe / 165
    Albuquerque / 201

RECOMMENDED READING / 209

Introduction for Parents and Other Grownups

Santa Fe is a marvelous town, filled with historic attractions, a lively assortment of arts events, plenty of good restaurants, world-class museums and even a little night life. Despite its well deserved reputation as a cultural outpost and sophisticated small town, Santa Fe also is a good place for children. Whether you're visiting for a few days or are lucky enough to live here, you'll find plenty of kid-friendly options. With 300 days of sunshine and only 14 inches of rain each year, Santa Fe's outdoor attractions are compelling and accessible.

Among the highlights:

- The city has a museum designed and constructed just for kids, complete with a special child-size door.
- Our indoor ice skating rink is open year-round and offers child-size skate rentals, lessons and more.
- Your kids will find two skateboard parks, basketball and tennis courts, swimming pools and bike trails. Classes in martial arts are available in private studios and at public recreation centers.
- The Museum of International Folk Art has an exhibit of dolls, toys and miniatures with special windows at a child's eye level. Afterwards, walk the labyrinth outside on adjoining Milner Plaza.

- The mountains and foothills surrounding Santa Fe are rich with opportunities for family picnics, hiking, horseback riding and mountain biking. You don't have to go far to take a river rafting trip, or find a spot to fish.
- In the winter, you and your kids can have fun together at Ski Santa Fe or with cross-country skiing or snowshoeing on trails in the Santa Fe National Forest or the Valles Caldera in the Jemez mountains. You can go sledding or tubing in Hyde Park.

Because Santa Fe boasts one of the country's most vibrant arts communities, our children benefit. Kids can study everything from painting and pottery to drama and dance in one-day programs offered through museums, by non-profit youth groups or commercial enterprises. Children can see professional theater, opera and music productions; some groups offer special concerts just for kids. The summer Spanish Market and Indian Markets, major arts and crafts shows, dedicate exhibition space to children who are also artists.

Many Santa Fe events include children in wonderful ways. The Fiesta de Santa Fe, a community celebration each September, invites kids to walk in their own parade. The pancake breakfast on the Fourth of July includes entertainment geared for families. And if Santa Fe, nicknamed "The City Different," seems a little too different at times, please realize that our community has all the comfortable standbys—library story hours, a mall where teens hang with friends, franchised and independent video rental outlets, theaters with Coke and popcorn, video game arcades and places for banana splits and snow cones.

The suggestions you'll find here are primarily intended for ages 5 to 12, although they often can be modified to suit younger or older children. We've included phone numbers (all area codes are

505) and websites for your convenience. If you have questions about hours or prices, please call ahead. Although we make every effort to keep *Children's Guide to Santa Fe* up to date, even we aren't perfect. Please let us know about your favorite Santa Fe sites by writing Children's Guide to Santa Fe, Anne Hillerman c/o Sunstone Press, Box 2321, Santa Fe, N.M. 87504-2321.

Enjoy your time in Santa Fe!

—Anne Hillerman

Introduction for Children

i there!

When I wrote this book, I thought about my son, Brandon, and what he liked when his Dad and I took him on vacation. He got grumpy if we spent our time in museums and bored when we went shopping. But he liked it when we went fishing or hiked to Indian caves or found a park with a waterslide or a basketball court.

So I used this book to answer what I remember as his favorite question: "What can I do here?"

There are plenty of fun things for children to do in Santa Fe. Santa Fe has a museum just for kids and lots of places for fishing, mountain biking and horse back riding. In the fall, there's a special parade for children and their pets. You and your grownups can use this book to find out about places to visit, things to do, and celebrations Santa Fe has each year that children find interesting.

I hope you'll enjoy this book and that it will help you have a good time here.

If you discover something in Santa Fe you really like that isn't in the book, could you let me know? You can write to me at Sunstone Press, Box 2321, Santa Fe, N.M. 87504-2321.

Thank you for reading.

—Anne Hillerman

FACTS ABOUT NEW MEXICO

State animal: Black Bear
State bird: Roadrunner (Chaparral)
State fish: Cutthroat Trout
State flower: Yucca
State gem: Turquoise
State motto: *Crescit Eundo* (It grows as it goes)
State nickname: Land of Enchantment
State songs: *O Fair New Mexico* by Elizabeth Garrett (English)
            Asi es Nuevo Mexico by Amadeo Lucero (Spanish)
State tree: Piñon
State vegetable: Chile
State question—Red or green? (Chile, that is!)

WANT TO LEARN MORE?

For more information on how you and your kids can have fun in Santa Fe, don't forget to check the local newspapers. *The Santa Fe New Mexican*, 995-3839, offers a Family Attractions category in its *Pasatiempo* calendar each Friday and *Best Bets for Kids*, on Thursdays. The daily *Albuquerque Journal Santa Fe*, 988-8881, and weekly *Santa Fe Reporter*, 988-5541, also include activities for children and families in their calendars. Two specialized free publications, *New Mexico Kids!*, 797-2708, and *Tumbleweeds*, 984-3171, present pages of ideas, suggestions and insights into services and activities for children in the Santa Fe areas. (All area codes are 505). And don't forget our Recommended Reading list at the end of this book.

Here are some sources for information on Santa Fe:

Santa Fe Convention & Visitors Bureau Information Center
Sweeney Center
201 W Marcy Street
Santa Fe, NM 87501
(800) 777-2489 or 955-6200
www.santafe.org

Santa Fe County Chamber of Commerce
8380 Cerrillos Road, Suite 302
Santa Fe, NM 87507
(505) 988-3279
www.santafechamber.com

City of Santa Fe
200 Lincoln Avenue
Santa Fe, NM 87501
City Government Information: 955-6500
www.santafenm.gov/index.asp

State of New Mexico Tourist Information Center
491 Old Santa Fe Trail
Santa Fe, NM 87501
(800) 733-6396 or 827-7307
www.newmexico.org

A TOUCH OF HISTORY

Heading West—The Old Santa Fe Trail brought settlers from the United States to Mexican Santa Fe. *Photograph by Don Strel*

Long before the Pilgrims landed at Plymouth Rock, Santa Fe was a busy town. From archaeological evidence, we know that Indians camped in the Santa Fe area on hunting trips for bison and other animals as long ago as 10,000 B.C. Eventually, the hunters established permanent annual camps in the area, and then came to live here year round. For about 800 years, Indians lived in and around what is now Santa Fe in pueblos, or villages made from adobe, or mud bricks. Some of their villages had hundreds of rooms and many plazas. Archaeologists believe that at least seven pueblos existed within a 20-minute drive of the spot where the Plaza now stands. In 2005, a pueblo was discovered beneath the city's Sweeney Convention Center! Sometime after A.D. 900, Indians built the Pueblo of Ogapoge, as it is called by tradition, on or near the current site of Santa Fe's Plaza. By the time the first Spanish arrived in the 16th century, however, Ogapoge was long abandoned.

Explorers from Spain came to this area looking for treasure as well as for a place to live. In the late 16th century, Juan de Onate set out for New Mexico. Accompanied by 129 soldiers and their families and a small group of friars, Onate camped at a spot about 25 miles north of what's now Santa Fe in 1598. Rather than living the easy life they'd hoped for, colonists had to work hard to survive. Many of them gave up and returned to Mexico. The Viceroy named a new governor, Pedro de Peralta, who moved the Spanish settlement to what is now Santa Fe, probably around 1608. Santa Fe is the oldest capital city in the United States.

As you do your own exploration of Santa Fe, you'll notice many signs of the Spanish ranchers and farmers, artists and soldiers who first came here. Some of the streets have Spanish names. Paseo de Peralta, Otero and De Vargas Streets honor Spanish explorers. Instead of roads and streets, you'll see *caminos* and *calles* in Santa Fe. The names are one way the people of Santa Fe recall their history.

The Pueblo Revolt

Santa Fe and New Mexico grew slowly as more colonists arrived and babies were born. As the Spanish colony grew, conflict began to fester. The Pueblo Indians were becoming increasingly unhappy with these newcomers. Initially, the Pueblo people accepted their new neighbors. But as the years went by, the Indians came to resent Spanish attempts to take away their religion, to impose Spanish culture in place of their traditional native ways, and to force them to work, including building Catholic churches. The Indians came up with a plan to drive the Spanish out, the Pueblo Revolt of 1680. It became the only successful revolution in the new world where native people drove away their colonists.

Runners with knotted ropes signifying the exact day of the revolt went from pueblo to pueblo, telling the Indian warriors that the time had come to send the Spanish out. Warriors burned the outlying churches and killed the priests and some Spanish settlers. Then they rode into Santa Fe, the center of the Spanish government. The settlers who could escape fled to the Palace of the Governors, a large building that was the headquarters of Spanish government. There, the outnumbered Spanish waited fearfully. During a nine-day siege the Indians burned Santa Fe's homes and crops and cut off the water supply to the Palace. Finally, the Spanish governor pledged that he and the remaining soldiers and settlers would leave, and the Indians let them go. A thousand settlers trudged back to Mexico.

For 12 years, Santa Fe and the rest of what is now New Mexico remained under Indian control. Spain viewed the loss of the territory as an embarrassment. In 1690, the king of Spain appointed Diego de Vargas as governor and charged him with reclaiming the territory. With a band of 40 Spanish soldiers and 50 Indians who had agreed to help, Vargas marched to Santa Fe. He convinced the Pueblo people to surrender and, on September 14, 1692, proclaimed Santa Fe and the rest of New Spain under his rule. The return of the Spanish is celebrated at the annual Fiestas de Santa Fe, one of the nation's oldest civic celebrations.

Although the re-conquest started peacefully, it took the Spanish years to reclaim the rest of New Mexico and many Indians and Spanish soldiers were killed. By 1696, however, the longest and most successful uprising of Native Americans against foreign colonists was over. Twenty-six Spanish governors followed Vargas. Some represented Spain with honor, wisdom and integrity; others were ignorant and corrupt. Santa Fe remained the territory's capital for the next 125 years and is now the state capital.

The Santa Fe Trail

Wagons Rolling—In addition to the Santa Fe Trail, depicted here by artist Sonny Rivera, settlers also came to Santa Fe from El Camino Real, which led north from Mexico. *Photograph by Don Strel*

Many people who have never been to Santa Fe have heard of the Santa Fe Trail, a famous wagon train route. Here's how it started:

In the late 18th century, Mexico gained independence from Spain. Santa Fe was now under Mexican rule. Unlike the Spanish, the Mexicans welcomed traders from the United States. Soon, great caravans of wagons rolled down the Santa Fe Trail, making a 900-mile trip from Missouri to the Santa Fe Plaza.

Santa Fe looked strange to these newcomers. Many didn't even recognize that small, brown buildings made from mud bricks were houses. Inside, the homes were different, too. Instead of beds, for instance, most families slept on mattresses which they folded to use as couches during the day. When the caravans returned they took hides and Indian weavings from New Mexico, and stories about Santa Fe, back to the United States.

In June 1846, New Mexicans learned that the United States had declared war on Mexico. U.S. General Stephen Watts Kearny and his staff rode into Santa Fe to meet with New Mexico's governor. The next day, Kearny told Santa Fe residents that they would now be ruled by the United States. In 1850, New Mexico became a U.S. territory. Santa Fe's residents, most of whom spoke only Spanish, adjusted to the U.S. presence and the number of American arriving every day. They called them *anglos*—a word they used to mean people who were not Spanish or American Indian.

Although most people don't realize it, the Civil War found Santa Fe. In February 1862, a Confederate general with troops from Texas invaded and took control of the city. About two weeks later, Union forces destroyed Confederate supplies and rebel forces headed south.

The Railroad, Statehood and Beyond

In the early 1880s, the railroad arrived in Santa Fe. The trains brought an end to the Santa Fe Trail and made travel between Santa Fe and cities in the east much easier. The trains delivered red bricks and other products that began to change the look of Santa Fe. Some people worried that Santa Fe would lose its unique adobe look, so a plan for Santa Fe's future was developed. The plan included rules for building to keep the city's old style.

Santa Fe residents led the fight for New Mexico statehood. Although three attempts at admission to the Union had failed, finally, on January 6, 1912, President William Howard Taft signed the bill making New Mexico the 47th state.

In 1916, an old fort was demolished to make way for the construction of the new Fine Arts Museum. A decade later, a group of artists and newcomers, headed by Will Schuster, breathed new life into the Santa Fe Fiesta, adding Zozobra, a giant flaming puppet, to the celebration which marked the return of Spanish settlers to the area centuries earlier. Santa Fe's art colony thrived. Painters captured the city's beauty on canvas and spread the word with their work.

In the 1940s New Mexico played a crucial role in the development of the atomic bomb. The U.S. government took over Los Alamos Ranch School in 1943, transforming it into a secret center for nuclear research. The project brought a steady stream of scientists and their families through Santa Fe. Atomic bombs built in Los Alamos were dropped on Nagasaki and Hiroshima. Los Alamos National Laboratory (LANL) does research today both in weapons and in topics such as energy, computer technology and space communication. Many people who work in Los Alamos live in Santa Fe.

In the 1950s and beyond, Santa Fe continued to grow. Plaza businesses began to cater more to tourists. The construction of the Santa Fe Opera in 1957 added to Santa Fe's appeal as an arts town. Beginning in the early 1980s, many Hollywood and music celebrities "discovered" Santa Fe, buying homes in the area and coming here on vacation. Modern Santa Fe's population reflects the city's deep roots. You'll find American Indian families, the descendents of the founding Spanish immigrants, great grandchildren of merchants who arrived over the Santa Fe Trail and new residents from California, Texas and elsewhere who enjoy the city's culture, history and natural environment

Have fun exploring our beautiful city.

Santa Fe Timeline

1150-1400—Pueblo Indian villages thrive along the Santa Fe River.

Early 15th century—Indians abandon the villages closest to Santa Fe.

1539—First Spanish exploration of New Mexico under Fray Marcos de Niza.

1540—Exploration and conquest of New Mexico by Coronado.

1598—Juan de Onate claims New Mexico for the Spanish and establishes the first Spanish settlement in New Spain near San Juan Pueblo northwest of Santa Fe.

1608-10—Pedro de Peralta establishes the city of Santa Fe as New Mexico's capital. The Palace of the Governors is built. El Camino Real runs from Mexico City to Santa Fe as a supply route for the Spanish missions and colony.

1680—The Pueblo Indians drive the Spanish out of Santa Fe and New Mexico.

1692—Diego de Vargas brings a Spanish military expedition back to Santa Fe and reclaims Santa Fe for the King of Spain.

1693-1696—Vargas returns to Santa Fe with a band of settlers. After a fierce battle, the Indians give up the Palace of the Governors.

1712—Santa Fe celebrates its first official Fiesta in thanksgiving for the reconquest.

1777–The first known map of Santa Fe is drawn.

1792–Pedro Vial blazes a trail from Santa Fe to St. Louis and returns the following year, making the first complete journey over what was to be known as the Santa Fe Trail.

1807–American explorer Zebulon Pike and his party are arrested as intruders in Spanish New Mexico. The Spanish government institutes measures to restrict American influence in New Spain, including Santa Fe.

1821–Mexico wins independence from Spain.

1822–The first wagons roll into the Santa Fe Plaza over the Santa Fe Trail, leading the way for millions of dollars of trade goods and new ideas and cultural influences in Santa Fe.

1833–The first gold mines west of the Mississippi open in the Ortiz Mountains between Santa Fe and Albuquerque.

1834–New Mexico's first newspaper, *El Crepusculo de la Libertad*, the Dawn of Liberty, is published in Santa Fe.

1837–A group of northern New Mexican farmers and Indians band together to protest new taxes imposed by the Mexican government. Governor Albino Perez is killed.

1846–The United States declares war on Mexico. U.S. General Stephen W. Kearny occupies Santa Fe without firing a shot.

1847–U.S. Territorial Gov. Charles Bent is assassinated in Taos. U.S. forces quell the rebellion in an attack that seriously damages the mission church at Taos Pueblo.

1848—The Treaty of Guadalupe Hidalgo is signed. Mexico cedes New Mexico to the United States.

1850—New Mexico becomes a U.S. territory.

1851—Santa Fe became the territorial capital and is incorporated as a city.

1851—The first English language school is founded in Santa Fe by Bishop Jean Lamy.

1851—A territorial library in founded in Santa Fe.

1861-62—Confederate soldiers from Texas invade Santa Fe and occupy the Palace of the Governors. The Battle of Glorieta, near Santa Fe, ends Confederate control in New Mexico.

1869—Construction of St. Francis Cathedral begins.

1874—Workers lay the foundations for Loretto Chapel.

1879—Governor Lew Wallace writes a portion of Ben Hur in the Palace of the Governors.

1880—The Atchison, Topeka & Santa Fe Railroad arrives in Santa Fe over a spur line from the main station in Lamy. Travel along the Santa Fe Trail dies away.

1881—Santa Fe installs its first water and telegraph systems.

1891—The City of Santa Fe is officially incorporated.

1907—The Palace of the Governors, saved from demolition, becomes a museum.

1912—New Mexico becomes the 47th state.

1917—The Museum of Fine Arts, another example of Santa Fe style, is dedicated.

1922—The Southwestern Association on Indian Affairs establishes the annual Indian market, a show that remains part of modern Santa Fe's cultural life.

1926—Artist Will Shuster creates Zozobra. The giant puppet quickly become a mainstay of the Santa Fe Fiesta.

1942—The federal government selects Los Alamos Boys School site for a secret project to develop an atomic bomb. Scientists and their families begin coming to Santa Fe on their way to the research site.

1957—John Crosby founds the Santa Fe Opera.

1960—Santa Fe celebrates its 350th anniversary.

1983—Santa Fe Community College is created.

1989—Santa Fe Children's Museum is founded.

1994—Debbie Jaramillo becomes Santa Fe's first woman mayor.

2000—Santa Fe peacefully welcomes the new millennium

2005—The revised *Children's Guide to Santa Fe* is published.

PLACES TO VISIT

n introduction

In this chapter you'll learn about some of Santa Fe's attractions. We'll start at the Plaza, the city's historic heart, and then tell you about other destinations in the city and on the outskirts. We've given addresses, phone numbers and websites for your information, so you can check on hours and admission fees. We've noted those places that are free to children.

In addition to this list, Santa Fe has other places of interest for children and families. For example, older children and those with special interest in art may enjoy visiting some of the city's many galleries. We have malls and commercial entertainment centers with video games, movie theaters and the like. Just look online or in a phone book.

You'll find places to visit outside of Santa Fe in our Day Trip section and more tips in the Get Movin' chapter.

All area codes are 505 unless indicated otherwise. If admission is free, or discounts are offered for children, we noted it.

Children Welcome—The Santa Fe Children's Museum offers a variety of activities, including animal encounters. *Photograph by Marjorie Young*

SANTA FE CHILDREN'S MUSEUM
1050 Old Pecos Trail, 989-8359
www.santafechildrensmuseum.org

A Safe Place—Children and parents can learn about animals, water, art and more at the Santa Fe Children's Museum. *Photograph by Marjorie Young*

How many towns offer kids their own museum? The Santa Fe Children's Museum is beloved by Santa Fe's resident youngsters and visitors as well. If you are traveling with kids younger than 12, plan to include at least half a day here on your Santa Fe agenda.

The museum focuses on hands-on activities in science and art. Preschoolers and early elementary-age children learn as they play here, and the museum's open concept allows parents to participate or watch as they choose. Children can splash and play in water while they learn to work a siphon and pump. They can climb through mirrored tunnels, and use magnets to build a bridge, tower, or a dragon. Don't miss the station for making giant bubbles, so big you can stand inside. The toddler climbing structure gives the smallest visitors a special place to explore. Older kids love the climbing wall. Once harnessed in and supported by a volunteer, they can use their body and mind to figure out how to maneuver to the top. Kids also enjoy the touchable animals here, including the snake and giant hissing cockroaches! Outdoors, the museum offers room to play and explore. You'll find a garden with fruit trees, a pond, musical installations and a miniature adobe village.

In addition to the exhibits, children can join a variety of hands-on programs with visiting scientists and artists. Special events include a summer Solstice Festival, the museum's birthday party and an annual ice cream social. The museum hosts parent education programs, special shows and workshops to coincide with school holiday breaks. Preschoolers get their own visiting times—no big kids allowed.

For parents, the museum hosts a popular Kids' Night Out. Mom and dad can drop off their children—ages 3 to 10—for dinner at the museum and a supervised evening of hands-on activities.

SANTA FE FARMERS' MARKET
Santa Fe Railyard, Cerrillos Road near Guadalupe Street
Santa Fe Rodeo Grounds, 3237 Rodeo Road
(at Richards Ave and at Ave Pueblos) 983-4098
www.farmersmarketsnm.org
Free admission

Flowers and Food—Santa Fe Farmers Market offers a variety of vegetables, fruit, plants, flowers and even entertainment.
Photograph by Ginger Wells courtesy Santa Fe Farmers' Market

If your kids think peas come from a can and carrots from a bag, a trip to the Santa Fe Farmers' Market will open their eyes and please their taste buds. Locals love the market, and many come early for the best selections and to meet their friends. On a Saturday at the height of the growing season, the market may draw 5,000 customers between opening at 7 a.m. and closing around noon—or when the vendors sell out.

You can see and buy fresh area produce, colorful cut flowers and baked treats here on Tuesdays and Saturdays, usually from mid-May until sometime in October. You'll find live music at the market most mornings, sometimes with children as part of the performance. Look for homemade salsa, herbal remedies, cheeses, organic meat, plants for landscaping and more. The farmers, about 110 or so at peak season, come from throughout northern New Mexico and elsewhere in the state. The market hosts special demonstrations and events and sponsors an annual tour to working farms.

In addition to the farmers, a crafts show is held on the grounds, with artisans showing a variety of hand-made work. An auxiliary farmers' market operates on Thursday afternoon and early evening at the Rodeo grounds usually from July through September.

During the winter, the market moves inside to El Museo Cultural, 1614 B Paseo Paseo de Peralta, and offers a more limited selection of green-house grown produce, meats and holiday gifts from the farm each Saturday. When you buy at any of the farmers' markets, you not only get delicious food, you're supporting small New Mexico businesses.

GEORGIA O'KEEFFE MUSEUM
217 Johnson Street, 995-0785
www.okeeffemuseum.org
Youth and students with ID free

The Georgia O'Keeffe Museum is America's first museum dedicated to the work of a woman artist of international stature. This private museum, a few blocks west of the Santa Fe Plaza, opened in 1997.

O'Keeffe visited New Mexico in 1917 and moved here permanently in 1949, settling in an old adobe home in the small village of Abiquiu. She lived there, inspired by the landscape and the light, for nearly 40 years before moving to Santa Fe a few years before her death in 1986 at age 98.

The Georgia O'Keeffe Museum houses the world's largest permanent collection of O'Keeffe's work, including many pieces the artist kept for herself that have never been exhibited previously. The museum displays drawings, paintings, pastels, sculptures and watercolors that O'Keeffe produced between 1916 and 1980. Flowers and bleached desert bones, abstractions, nudes, landscapes, cityscapes and still lifes were all subjects of interest to her. The museum also collects works by contemporaries of O'Keeffe who were part of her artistic community. The museum offers guided tours, educational programming, special events and also features a short video about O'Keeffe's life and her contribution to American art.

The museum offers educational opportunities for children and families. The staff and guest artists conduct a free hands-on learning experience each month to explore ideas and themes found in current exhibitions. Children ages 5-12 and their parents are invited to discover pertinent themes in art by looking at works on exhibit in the galleries and participating in multi-disciplinary art activities. Designed to engage both children and adults, the activities promote critical thinking and creative, interdisciplinary art making. The two-hour sessions are a fun family outing and offer follow-up activities to do at home.

INSTITUTE OF AMERICAN INDIAN ARTS MUSEUM
108 Cathedral Place, 983-1777
www.iaiancad.org
Children under 16 free

This museum shows Indian art through Indian eyes. One of the highlights of the collection is the National Collection of Contemporary Indian Art, an assembly of paintings, sculpture, photographs, drawings, prints and other works on paper, textiles, costumes, baskets, jewelry, pottery, ceramics, and beadwork. With more than 6,500 pieces in the collection representing 3,000 artists, the museum is the largest repository of contemporary Indian art in the world.

The museum has five galleries and the outdoor Allan Houser Art Park where you'll find large sculpture and room for the kids to relax. The museum is affiliated with the Institute of American Indian Arts, a leading Native American art school with a campus on the south side of town.

The museum occupies an historic Pueblo Revival style building just across the street from St. Francis Cathedral Basillica. The IAIA recently received a grant from the National Park Service's Save America's Treasures program for a much needed structural renovation of the building, listed in the National Register of Historic Places. The renovation was designed to enhance the building's structural integrity and to improve the overall environmental quality of the facility. The work was completed in the summer of 2005.

LIBRARIES
Santa Fe Public Libraries:

Main Library, 145 Washington Avenue 955-6780
La Farge Branch, 1730 Llano Street, 955-4860
Bookstop, Santa Fe Place 955-2980.
www.santafelibrary.org

Vista Grande Public Library
14 Avenida Torreon (El Dorado), 466-7323
Free

In the children's rooms at these libraries, you'll find books for children as well as story hours and other special events. Both the downtown and LaFarge libraries have children's rooms with child-size shelving and seating. The book collection covers a broad range of fiction and non-fiction titles. In addition to regular story hours for pre-schoolers, the libraries other programs that encourage reading.

The Bookstop, located in the Santa Fe Place, offers a fine opportunity to combine reading with a shopping trip. A growing collection of books in Spanish for adults and children is available at the main library and the branches.

Children's librarians at Main and La Farge provide activities for youngsters three years old through grade school. Weekly story times for pre-school children ages three to six are presented throughout the year, as well as special programs for school-age children. Summer programs provide both entertainment and information and encourage reading with contests and a variety of other activities. The programs are free but children need to sign up for them at the library they use most often.

The libraries' Reading Buddies program provides one-to-one reading assistance and practice for school-age students (ages 7 and up). Volunteers, helpers and readers sign up to work with the program in the spring and receive some training.

Santa Fe's public library system began in 1896, when the Women's Board of Trade and Library Association set up a reading room near the Plaza. On January 13, 1908, the first Santa Fe Public Library opened at 120 Washington Ave., just across the street from the current downtown library. When the city needed a more spacious main library, the site chosen was the Berardinelli Building, a former city hall designed by John Gaw Meem in 1936. On January 17, 1987, a beautiful new home for books at 145 Washington Avenue was opened to the public.

The La Farge Branch was opened on December 3, 1978 to serve the city's expanding southwest sector. The Bookstop Library opened at Villa Linda Mall, now the Santa Fe Place, in the spring of 1988, first to serve as a temporary facility while the La Farge Branch was renovated and then as a permanent storefront library. Santa Fe plans a new south-side library to open in July, 2006.

The Santa Fe Public Library is a division of the Community Services Department of the City of Santa Fe. It is primarily funded by city revenues and supplemented by funds from the Friends of the Library, the New Mexico State Library, private donations and grants.

The Vista Grande Public Library in Eldorado, southeast of Santa Fe, is not part of the Santa Fe Public Library system, but was partly funded by Santa Fe County. It opened its children's room in 2004. The room is named in honor of Irene S. Peck, New Mexico's first State Librarian. The library offers children's summer and after school reading programs.

MUSEUM OF FINE ARTS
107 W. Palace Ave., 476-5072
www.mfasantafe.org
Free admission for children 16 and younger

Children with an interest in art might enjoy a look at the state's oldest art museum, the Museum of Fine Arts. The museum features more than 20,000 works of art from the Southwest. Completed in 1917, the museum is a beautiful example of the Pueblo Revival style of construction, complete with split cedar *latillas* (roof supports), hand hewn *vigas* (log roof beams) and corbels. The gracious look reflected in the thick walls, pleasantly landscaped central courtyard, smooth interior plaster and other finishing touches became synonymous with "Santa Fe Style." The Museum's St. Francis Auditorium is used for concerts and other public events throughout the year.

The museum houses paintings, photography, sculpture, and other art. Many of the works focus on the American Southwest of the 20th century. The museum offers Art Walking Tours of Santa Fe spring through fall, highlighting the art and architectural history of downtown Santa Fe.

MUSEUM OF INDIAN ARTS & CULTURE/ LABORATORY OF ANTHROPOLOGY
710 Camino Lejo, 476-1250
www.miaclab.org
Free admission for children 16 and younger

Children Welcome—Puzzles are part of the fun at the Discovery Center, a special place for children at the Museum of Indian Arts and Culture.
Photo courtesy Museum of Indian Arts and Culture Education Division

Here, among the museum's many exhibits, children especially enjoy "Here, Now and Always." This exhibit includes more than 1,300 objects and a multimedia production to tell the story of the Native American presence in the Southwest. Visitors can hear recorded voices of contemporary American Indians in a clever design that brings centuries of culture and tradition to life. You can step into a Pueblo kitchen, an Apache *wickiup*, a Navajo *hogan*, a 1930s trading post and a contemporary vendor's booth at a tribal feast day celebration.

The museum also has a Discovery Center where kids can learn about Native American culture through hands-on fun. The themed areas of the Discovery Center highlight stories, archaeology, weaving, rock art, and architecture.

While you're visiting the museum, take a look at the sculpture garden outside and the huge sculpture of an Apache dancer at Milner Plaza, the central area that connects this museum with the Museum of International Folk Art at the other end. The Plaza has a labyrinth that many children enjoy walking.

MUSEUM OF INTERNATIONAL FOLK ART
706 Camino Lejo, 476-1200
www.moifa.org
Free admission for children 16 and younger

Family Fun—At the Museum of International Folk Art, parents and children will find delightful exhibits and a varied program of activities. *Photograph courtesy Museum of New Mexico*

Except for the Children's Museum, of all Santa Fe's museums this one holds the most interest for young visitors.

You may be surprised to learn that the Museum of International Folk Art has the world's largest collection of international folk art. Don't miss "Multiple Visions: A Common Bond," which displays toys, dolls and objects from more than 100 countries—more than 10,000 pieces of folk art! The collection comes to life in dioramas that replicate market scenes, rowdy festivals, dinner parties, a funeral, a bullfight and other slices of daily life. Children can peek in through windows at just the right height for them to see the scenes inside.

The Hispanic Heritage Wing features Spanish Colonial folk art and an interactive computer program in its *Familia y Fe*/Family and Faith exhibit. The Museum's Neutrogena Collection comprises more than 2,500 textiles, ceramics and carvings from all over the world. Lloyd's Treasure Chest allows children to open drawers filled with surprises and see videos about artists and their works.

Along with regular programs of changing and interactive exhibitions, the museum hosts a menu of activities for children and families during the summer and in conjunction with its exhibits. Many museum events are free. The museum also has a family-friendly lounge area with couches, books for children about folk art, puppets, toys and a train set. It's the ideal place for resting tired kids and tired feet.

MUSEUM OF SPANISH COLONIAL ART
750 Camino Lejo, 982-2226
www.spanishcolonial.org
Free admission for children 16 and younger

Spanish Colonial Discovery—The Museum of Spanish Colonial Art includes items from daily life in New Mexico in days past and a hands-on section for children.
Photographs by Bill Field courtesy Museum of Spanish Colonial Art

This private museum celebrates the resourcefulness and skill of Spanish colonial artists past and present. It is exclusively dedicated to preserving, interpreting and promoting Spanish Colonial art forms and features the world's largest collection of art from the colonial era of Spain.

Special attractions for kids include the 'Possible Bag' with coloring pages, a puzzle and creative activities to personalize their visit and focus attention on different objects of art. Children as young as four can participate in a treasure hunt and win a prize. The Youth Art and Activity Gallery includes reproductions of period clothing children can try on. All activities are free with museum admission, which is free for children 16 and younger. The museum also sponsors educational outreach programs in public and private schools and art centers in the Santa Fe area.

Spanish Colonial Exhibits – The museum offer a glimpse at the daily lives of the unique Hispano cultures that thrive around the world today. Among its attractions, the museum has a small gallery of youth artwork which is also an interactive area for art activities.
Photo by Bill Field, courtesy Museum of Spanish Colonial Art

PALACE OF THE GOVERNORS
105 West Palace Avenue (on the Plaza), 476-5100
www.palaceofthegovernors.org
Free admission for children 16 and younger

Constructed in the early 17th century as Spain's seat of government for what is today the American Southwest, the Palace of the Governors doesn't look anything like the palaces of Europe. However, this simple adobe (mud brick) building is a treasure house of the history of Santa Fe, New Mexico and the Spanish Southwest.

The exhibits, collections and archives include the Spanish colonial days (1540-1821), the brief Mexican period (1821-1846), U.S. Territorial times (1846-1912) and from statehood to the present. Visitors to the Palace can see storage bins from 1693 in a glass-covered pit beneath the floor boards—discovered during archaeological excavation. Also of interest are the Segesser Hides, paintings done in the early 18th century by Indians to record the activities of the Spanish and French. The museum has compelling displays of material from the Santa Fe Trail and the Civil War in New Mexico.

Each year before Christmas, the museum hosts a special celebration of songs and stories of the season. In October, 2004, construction began on a new museum to celebrate New Mexico history.

PALACE OF THE GOVERNORS PORTAL
Portal artists—a living exhibit
105 W. Palace Avenue (on the Plaza), 476-5100
www.newmexicoindianart.org
Free

Palace Portal—Native American artists from throughout northern and central New Mexico sell their creations in the shade of the Palace of the Governors Portal. *Photograph by Don Strel*

Beneath the long portal along the south side of the Palace of the Governors sit Native American artists and craftspeople who sell their handmade goods to tourists and locals almost every day of the year, rain or shine. The Indians are recognized as a living "exhibit," chosen by lottery from artists who have applied to sell here. They represent 41 tribes, pueblos, chapters and villages in New Mexico, the Navajo Nation, and parts of Arizona.

To be accepted, a person's work has to be authentic and handmade using traditional materials. The portal artists display a wide selection of fine work, both traditional and contemporary in design. In the summer, some of the artists bring their own kids. These artists and craftspeople are part of a decades-old tradition. If they aren't too busy, the vendors may talk to you about how they make what they sell.

Native American artists and craftspeople sell their work at the Palace of the Governors from 8 a.m. to dusk. Prices range from a few dollars to many hundreds depending on the item. Sometimes vendors may also bring cookies, small fruit pies and homemade bread for sale.

THE PLANETARIUM
Santa Fe Community College, upper level, west wing
6401 Richards Avenue, 428-1677
www.sfccnm.edu/sfcc/pages/914.html
Discounted tickets for children; not appropriate for those under 5

Attractions of the night sky get the focus here with movies, lectures, theater presentations, concerts, star parties and free telescope viewing. Programs range from scientific documentaries and stories filled with science facts to presentations that focus on Native American stories of the sky, or offer a look at sky lore from other cultures. In the live shows, trained staff members take visitors on a trip through the stars. One of the most popular programs, Celestial Highlights, provides an introduction to the stars and constellations that will be visible for the next 30 days.

All children must be accompanied by an adult and most programs are not suitable for children younger than 5 years old. Tucked away on the community college campus, the planetarium is away from the usual tourist stops, but worth a trip.

EL RANCHO DE LAS GOLONDRINAS
334 Los Pinos Road, La Cienega, 15 miles south of Santa Fe.
471-2261
www.golondrinas.org
Admission charge varies by event.

Spanish Dancers—El Rancho de las Golondrinas, the Ranch of the Swallows, is a living history museum which offers a variety of exhibits and special programs.
Photograph courtesy El Rancho de las Golondrinas

El Rancho de las Golondrinas, a living history museum, sits on 200 acres in a rural farming valley just south of Santa Fe. A visit to this ranch, named for the *golondrinas* or swallows which nest here, is a step into New Mexico's Spanish Colonial history. The ranch was the last stop before Santa Fe on the long route up from Mexico City.

At the ranch you can see the fort the King of Spain ordered built to protect the ranch against Indians. You'll feel the heat in a blacksmith shop and the cool shade provided by ancient cottonwood trees. You'll hear the rush of water over a wooden waterwheel that powers the mill and notice the stillness in the old *morada,* or chapel. At the pond you might hear frogs and see iridescent dragonflies. During the summer, Las Golondrinas is a busy place with a variety of special events nearly every weekend. The ranch is open several days a week from early summer until September. (Please see our Events section for more information.)

The ranch includes original colonial buildings from the early 18th century and other historic buildings brought in from other places of northern New Mexico and reassembled at Las Golondrinas. All have been furnished as you would have seen them if you'd been alive back then. Don't miss the little school house, complete with a dunce cap!

If you visit the ranch during the spring or fall festivals, you'll find that it has come to life. Volunteers clothed in the styles of the times spin yarn, shoe horses, bake bread, tend the animals, chat with visitors, and recreate every day life in early New Mexico. You'll also discover music, dancing, costumed riders on horseback, food and arts and crafts for sale.

When you visit, be prepared to do some walking. The museum's self-guided tour involves about a 1.5-mile walk over roads and trails that are sometimes steep and rocky and hard on baby strollers.

SHIDONI FOUNDRY, INC.
PO Box 250, Tesuque, 988-8001
www.shidoni.com
Free

Even kids who've never thought much about art love to play in this spacious sculpture garden and see the bronze pouring.

The wonderful sculptures, many of them larger than life-size, sit among cottonwoods and apple trees inviting visitors to stroll among them and take a photograph. Visitors have the opportunity to watch 2000 degree molten bronze being poured into ceramic shell molds. (Please call for pouring times). Also on the property, the Shidoni art gallery, which represents a wide variety of sculpture from all over the country, may be of interest to older kids and parents. The foundry is open for self-guided tours and bronze pours occur year around, both at no charge.

"Shidoni" is a Navajo word used as a greeting to a friend.

The foundry and sculpture garden are on Bishop's Lodge Road, five miles north of the Santa Fe Plaza.

WHEELWRIGHT MUSEUM OF THE AMERICAN INDIAN
704 Camino Lejo, 982-4636 or (800) 607-4636
www.wheelwright.org
Free

Built in 1937, this museum is shaped like an eight-sided Navajo *hogan*. Privately operated, the museum was founded by Mary Cabot Wheelwright, a wealthy woman from Boston, and Hastiin Klah, a Navajo medicine man. Changing exhibitions feature historic and contemporary Native American art and culture with an emphasis on Southwestern tribes.

The Wheelwright Museum usually offers a main exhibit with various types of art and small exhibits which spotlight individual Native American artists or contain items related to the main show. The museum offers many free events throughout the year, including storytelling, children's reading hours, a major children's powwow, lectures, gallery tours and talks about Native American art.

Of special interest to children is the museum's shop, The Case Trading Post, built to resemble a turn-of-the-century Navajo Reservation trading post. It's a fine place to shop. Don't miss it. In addition to a large inventory of authentic, Indian-made arts and crafts and a fine collection of books, the trading post gives visitors a feeling of having stepped directly into the past.

Arts and Culture

n introduction

Children and teens with an interest in the arts, from dance to drawing, will find plenty of opportunities in Santa Fe. The city offers many programs, some free or on a sliding scale, a few of which are listed here. In addition to what you'll find in this book, nearly all of Santa Fe's public and private museums offer classes, workshops or special programs for children and families from time to time. You can find information about them in the our Places to Visit chapter. Many professional music groups have outreach programs or special discounts for children at concerts. Visiting dance companies may offer young artists workshops. The area's colleges—Santa Fe Community College, St. John's College and the College of Santa Fe—often feature classes for kids through their continuing education programs as well as summer or school break camps. You'll find special arts-related activities for kids and families throughout the year.

Many studies have shown that exposure to the arts helps children learn other things as well. And besides that, being in a play, dancing, making a collage, building a pot, taking a photograph or sketching a cartoon is a proven source of great fun. Enjoy!

If you're outside of New Mexico and want to call one of the places listed here for information, remember that all area codes are 505 unless indicated otherwise.

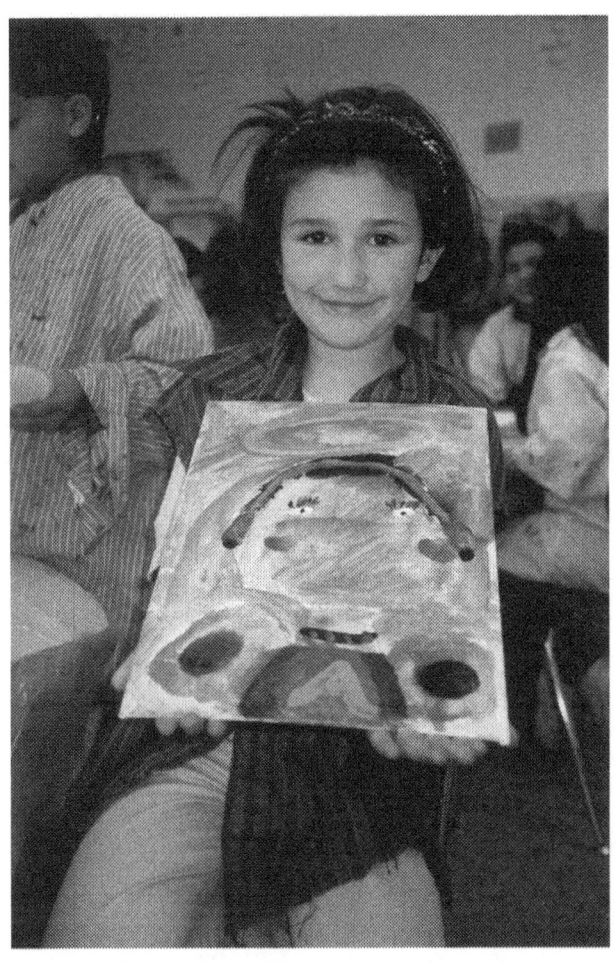

Art for Everyone—Santa Fe has a tremendous variety of arts programs for children, from visual art to dance, music, theater and more.
Photograph courtesy Fine Arts for Children and Teens

ARTS ALIVE ON MILNER PLAZA
Milner Plaza and Museum of International Folk Art, 706 Camino Lejo, 476-1200
www.moifa.org

Milner Plaza—An oasis between the museums on Camino Lejo, the plaza hosts a variety of lively family events. *Photograph by Eliza Wells Smith courtesy Museum of New Mexico*

Arts Alive on Milner Plaza is a happy, creative series of outdoor events for Santa Fe residents and their visitors, all for free. The hands-on programs happen during July and August each summer, usually two afternoons a week. The events are often tied to exhibits at the museum. In connection with the 2005 Carnaval! exhibit, for example, the museum offered Arts Alive workshops on mask making and cape construction. All sessions are open to children and adults with no materials fee or even advance registration required. Other topics have included weaving activities co-sponsored by the museum and the Española Valley Fiber Arts group.

ASPEN SANTA FE BALLET
550-B St. Michael's Drive, 983-5591
www.aspensantafeballet.com

Ballet—Aspen Santa Fe Ballet is one of many options for children who want to study dance. *Photograph by Claire Lighton courtesy Aspen Santa Fe Ballet*

The school of Aspen Santa Fe Ballet offers year-round training for both recreational and pre-professional ballet students. It is the only ballet school in New Mexico affiliated with a nationally recognized professional dance company. Instruction focuses on fostering confidence and individual accomplishments as well as developing technique and artistry.

During the Summer Intensive, designed for dancers ages 11 to 18, master teachers are invited to teach in a three week pre-professional program. The children's summer workshop, usually held in June for ages 8-13, offers daily ballet classes as well as folk dance and jazz. The school also offers creative movement classes for children ages 3-6 and afterschool and Saturday classes in creative movement, ballet, tap, jazz and modern dance during the school year.

In addition to classroom work, the school provides students with the opportunity to perform in a production of The Nutcracker each winter along side the professional dancers in the company.

Limited scholarship funds are available. School of Aspen Santa Fe Ballet alumni have danced with the New York City Ballet, Washington Ballet, Pittsburgh Ballet Theater and others.

FINE ARTS FOR CHILDREN & TEENS (FACT)
1516 Pacheco Street, 992-2787
www.factsantafe.org

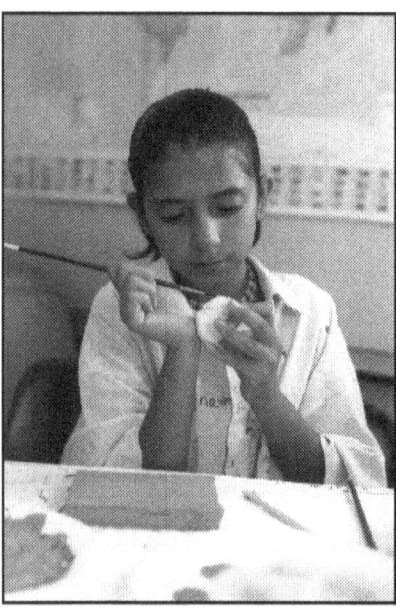 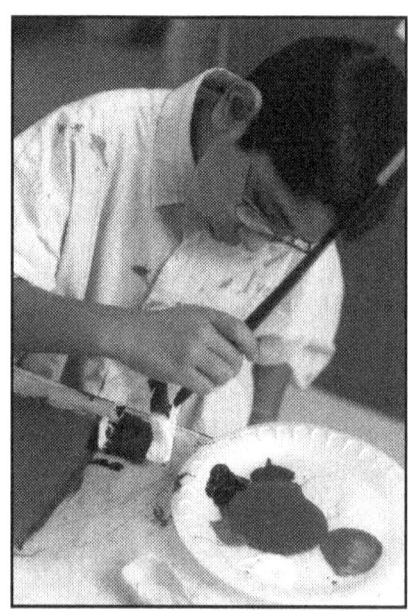

Draw, Paint and More—Fine Arts for Children and Teens offers classes after school and during the summer and also works with teachers to help them use the arts in their classes. *Photograph by Jennifer Espinosa courtesy Fine Arts for Children and Teens*

This visual arts program, started in 1990, offers after school programs and summer classes in the schools and at FACT's home, the ARTbarn. Classes in drawing, painting, sculpture, collage and more are available for ages 4 to 18. Among the activities is a summer show of student artwork and art classes at the city's Genoveva Chavez Community Center.

Older children with an interest in teaching may be invited to work with the younger kids in a mentor program which uses teens as studio assistants. FACT also provides internships for college art education majors. In addition to art-making, FACT programs are designed to empower and transform children by teaching leadership, literacy and life skills. Sliding scale tuition and scholarships are available.

In addition to its direct work with kids, FACT offers workshops to help classroom teachers integrate art into their curriculum. A nonprofit organization, FACT is funded by foundations, businesses and private donors. The group has received several grants from the National Endowment for the Arts.

GIRLSFILMSCHOOL
College of Santa Fe, 1600 St. Michael's Drive, 473-6409
www.girlsfilmschool.csf.edu

GirlsFilmSchool, a two-week residential summer film program for teen girls at the College of Santa Fe, offers 20 girls from around the country a chance to learn the basics of film, video and performance from both sides of the camera. The program is open to girls who have completed their sophomore, junior or senior year in high school.

Students spend their days in the college's Garson Communications Center, learning from guest artists, College of Santa Fe faculty and an enthusiastic group of mentors—upperclasswomen in the college's Moving Image Arts Department. Several GirlsFilmSchool graduates return each year to serve as peer mentors. The program offers a public screening series each year to introduce up-and-coming filmmakers to the Santa Fe community and generate interest in the program.

Funding for GirlsFilmSchool comes from the National Endowment for the Arts, the Academy of Motion Picture Arts & Sciences Foundation as well as many local and area donors. The financial support goes toward program costs and financial aid; about half of the participants receive full or partial scholarships.

The film school introduces students to basic concepts of writing for film, producing, acting, interviewing, editing, video production techniques and web site design. Evening screenings offer the girls an opportunity to view a wide variety of work by professional women in the moving image arts. Several of these women filmmakers join the girls to discuss their work.

INSTITUTE FOR SPANISH ARTS
1516 Pacheco Street, PO Box 8418, Santa Fe, NM 87505-8418,
995-8562
www.mariabenitez.com

Internationally-acclaimed as a performer, choreographer and director in the flamenco world, Santa Fe's Maria Benitez established the Institute for Spanish Arts here in part to work with children. The Institute offers programs for youngsters after school and in the summer. The dancers also present free concerts in the public schools.

The Institute faculty teaches three levels of Spanish dance classes for young students along with creative movement for ages 4-7, ballet and guitar lessons. At the end of the summer program the children have an opportunity to display their new skills in a public performance on the Plaza in Santa Fe in celebration of the city's Fiesta. Benitez designed the summer children's program to enhance the public's awareness of Spanish/Hispanic arts and culture and to give the children of Santa Fe and surrounding communities a creative alternative for self-expression and fun.

Since 2001 the Institute has offered fall after school classes for children to continue their study of Spanish dance and guitar year-round. The curriculum is taught by members of the Estampa Española professional dance company. Each nine-week class session includes an open student recital. Scholarships are available.

THE LENSIC, SANTA FE'S PERFORMING ARTS CENTER
211 West San Francisco Street
Box Office: 988-1234, Ticket information: 988-7050
www.lensic.com

From jazz to comedy, from classic movies to renowned lecturers and acrobats, The Lensic Performing Arts Center brings entertainment of all kinds to the heart of Santa Fe. Located downtown across from the public parking garage, the Lensic includes many family appropriate artists in its schedule of performances and productions.

The historic theater, built as a vaudeville house and cinema in 1931, regained its former glory during a major renovation in 2001 and now plays gracious host to roughly 250 performances every year: theater, music, dance, poetry and film. Comfy chairs and an expansive balcony make for a house full of good seats. Clever programming brings a sold-out show with frequency.

The Lensic's schedule is printed in the local newspapers, or you can stop by the theater when you're downtown to see what's coming up.

LOS ALAMOS CONCERT ASSOCIATION
PO Box 572, Los Alamos, 662-9000
www.losalamos.org/laca

This long-established non-profit organization usually presents five visiting artists in concerts during the fall, winter and spring. Performances are held in the Duane Smith Auditorium on the Los Alamos High School campus, 1300 Diamond Dr. Best of all, people under 18 years of age are admitted free at concerts presented by The Los Alamos Concert Association.

Preceding the performances, the artist or artists usually present a pre-concert lecture and the audience is invited to a reception for the artist following the concert. The programs usually include solo artists and group performances by leading musicians from throughout the country and around the world.

THE NATIONAL DANCE INSTITUTE OF NEW MEXICO
1140 Alto Street, 983-7646
www.ndi-nm.org

Statewide Outreach—The National Dance Institute of New Mexico, based in Santa Fe, uses dance in the public schools to teach teamwork, confidence and other skills.
Photograph courtesy National Dance Institute

Founded with the knowledge that the arts have a unique power to engage and motivate children, this distinctive dance program helps children develop discipline, a standard of excellence and a belief in themselves that is likely to carry over into all aspects of their lives.

Since its start in Santa Fe in 1990, NDI has taught thousands of children in more than 70 schools throughout New Mexico. Annual performances reach diverse audiences of 52,000 parents, students and community members. NDI-NM is the only statewide arts education organization in New Mexico.

NDI-NM's performance style is a mix of dance and athletics, with many of the same benefits as a good physical education program. Each class is taught by a certified NDI-NM teacher and accompanied by a professional pianist. School-based classes are non-intimidating for non-dancers, and designed to be fun.

The in-school program places a dance instructor, an assistant instructor and pianist in elementary schools for the entire school year where they work with the same group of children every week. Children perform in a school-wide, interactive assembly in December and in community-wide performances involving hundreds of children from all participating schools who dance for an audience of parents, teachers, friends and neighbors.

In addition to the in-school programs, NDI-NM offers after-school training geared to children and teens wanting advanced dance instruction. These programs include after-school classes and the Santa Fe and Albuquerque Summer Institutes. NDI also sponsors a summer dance intensive for intermediate and advanced dancers, ages 14 to 20. The institute offers training in ballet, tap, jazz and singing. NDI-NM has a wide range of sliding scale scholarships based on financial need.

O'KEEFFE ART AND LEADERSHIP PROGRAMS
Georgia O'Keeffe Museum
217 Johnson Street, 995-0785
www.okeeffemuseum.org

The O'Keeffe Art and Leadership Program for Girls is an interactive outreach program which incorporates new skills and solving problems to enhance creativity and self-esteem. The program exposes the girls to women artists as role models. The program encourages participating students to have high aspirations and set goals for themselves. In addition to providing an intensive summer experience, the leadership program continues with activities throughout the school year. College and high school interns and women with careers in the arts work with Santa Fe girls, ages 11 through 13, who are nominated by teachers, counselors, and artists.

A similar project, the Art and Leadership Program for Boys, uses male museum staff, interns, and artists experienced in gender-based learning to lead the program and serve as role models.

Both programs offer the participants the opportunity to participate in an exhibition, usually in August, which presents a sampling of students' drawing, painting, sculpture, video, mixed media, poetry, creative writing, dance and theater.

In addition to the children who participate, the leadership program also benefits the teenagers and young adults who serve as mentors. High school and college interns who work with the children are selected from applicants nationally. Program interns have been chosen from the Institute of American Indian Arts, Bard College, University of North Carolina at Chapel Hill, Colorado State University and elsewhere. Not only do the interns enrich the learning experiences for the participants, the older students report personal growth and awareness and the acquisition of meaningful work skills as a result of helping with the program.

SANTA FE CHAMBER MUSIC FESTIVAL
239 Johnson Street, 983-2075
www.sfcmf.org

Musical Exploration—This percussion ensemble from the Santa Fe Chamber Music Festival entertained children and adults alike on the Plaza.
Photograph by Chris Nailor courtesy Santa Fe Chamber Music Festival

The Santa Fe Chamber Music Festival, a long-established summer arts organization, has an extensive program of music in the schools, free open rehearsals and youth concerts.

The Festival's summer youth concert series brings the magic of chamber music to life for children and their families in an interactive and educational way. The presentations are designed to engage young people in a musical experience that leaves them with a new curiosity and knowledge about the world of music. Presented by Festival artists, the summer series offers a variety of musical experiences from classical to jazz, drawing directly from the Festival's regular programming. Concerts are usually held at St. Francis Auditorium in the Museum of Fine Arts.

The festival's daytime rehearsals are also open free to the public, providing an informal look into the dynamics of performances and artists. Rehearsals are held at St. Francis Auditorium in the Museum of Fine Arts and the Lensic Performing Arts Center. The Festival posts weekly schedules at the venues once the season begins or offers them by phone.

Outside the concert hall, the Music in Our Schools program provides Santa Fe Public Elementary School students with the opportunity to hear live chamber music performances right in their school building. The program introduces young listeners to chamber music and enhances their appreciation for other types of music as well. Festival ensembles perform four different programs at each of the participating schools throughout the year. The Festival works with music teachers to develop lesson plans that prepare the children for ensemble performances and reinforce concepts afterwards.

SANTA FE COMMUNITY ORCHESTRA
551 W. Cordova Rd. #211, 466-4879
www.sfco.org

All Santa Fe Community Orchestra's programs are family friendly, and admission is free! The SFCO presents five concerts a year between October and June on Sunday afternoons in St. Francis Auditorium in the Museum of Fine Arts. The musicians perform the classics including works by Beethoven, Mozart, Tchaikovsky and Bartok, and accessible contemporary works by composers such as Torke, Pärt, Adams, and Rautavaara. Recent seasons have also featured popular, large choral works such as Beethoven's *Ninth Symphony* and Orff's *Carmina Burana*.

Before the concert, the "Anatomy of a Symphony" presentations preview the program with stories by SFCO Music Director Oliver Prezant and musical illustrations from the orchestra. The talks are a great introduction to symphonic music and an easy way to learn more about the orchestra, what a composer does and how the musicians prepare for a concert.

The orchestra also performs one or two free youth concerts every season in places such as a public school, the Santa Fe Childrens Museum, Stieren Hall at the Santa Fe Opera, and the Santa Fe Indian School. The group hosts free instrument-making workshops and the Pictures at an Exhibition Project which teaches about the relationship between music and visual art. SFCO has a "New Works by New Mexico's Composers" program which features readings of new pieces presented in an open rehearsal format. Submissions from young composers have been presented, such as the *Adagio for Orchestra* by Gabriel Gonzales, a high school student from Santa Fe.

Although the concerts are open to all, the organizers encourage families to use common sense about bringing very young children. As at all concerts, dance programs and plays, everyone needs to listen quietly without fidgeting or chatting.

SANTA FE NEW MUSIC
PO Box 6986, Santa Fe, 87502, 474-6601
www.sfnm.org

Youth Fest—Young musicians have a chance to perform with Santa Fe New Music. *Photograph courtesy Santa Fe New Music*

Established in 2000, Santa Fe New Music's youth education programs offer opportunities for study and performance for young people in the Santa Fe area. Santa Fe New Music also stages an annual free family concert in the Santa Fe area.

The SFNM Youth Ensemble is one of the nation's only youth ensembles dedicated exclusively to the study and performance of 20th and 21st century classical music. The group welcomes proficient musicians ages 11 to18 who would like to learn new music scores and perform them at SFNM Youthfest and other events. Participation is free.

In its annual New Mexico Young Composers' Project, SFNM accepts scores from composers age 18 and younger throughout New Mexico. The competition offers an opportunity for professional review of their compositions and a cash prize. There is no entry fee. To support the composers' project, SFNM hosts Young Composer Workshops in score preparation in Santa Fe and Albuquerque. The workshops are open to any young composer, not just those interested in participating in the competition.

In 2005, SFNM presented its first "Hands and Ears On" workshop in reading and playing new music. Designed for young musicians who want to learn about contemporary and experimental music, the workshop explores different styles, graphic scores and improvisation. Young people hear, perform and compose new music—all of which is intended to enhance their musical experience.

The SFNM Youth Ensemble also performs school concerts.

SANTA FE OPERA
Youth Nights at the Opera and other programs
Santa Fe Opera Theater
7 miles north of the downtown Santa Fe Plaza on U.S. 84/285, 986-5955.
www.santafeopera.org/commprograms/youthnites.php

Opera Made Easy—The Santa Fe Opera offers programs for children and families to make opera accessible and fun. *Photograph by Scott Humbert courtesy Santa Fe Opera*

The Santa Fe Opera offers several free or low-cost outreach programs for children and their parents.

Youth Nights at the Opera enables families to attend final dress rehearsals of several operas at greatly reduced prices. Each rehearsal is fully staged and costumed with full orchestral accompaniment—just like the real thing! As in regular performances, opera titles provide translations of the words the singers are singing in both English and Spanish on small screens in front of every seat. Families, especially those who haven't been to an opera before, are encouraged to attend the 30-minute informal pre-opera lectures in Stieren Orchestra Hall adjacent to the opera theater. Audience participation is encouraged during the lively talks.

To keep grownups from hogging the fun, tickets for Youth Nights are sold only in packages—one adult and two children or two adults and three children with tickets available for additional children or young adults, ages 15 to 22. Young adults may also purchase tickets on their own.

The opera also offers:

- Comprehensive, behind-the-scenes back-stage tours which give children and adults an opportunity to take a peak at the makings of opera. The walking tour includes scene storage areas, the costume shop, prop shop and production areas. Tours usually begin in July are offered each afternoon, Monday through Saturday, through the last Saturday in August. The one-hour tour is free for children ages 5 to 17.
- Each summer, children and their elders from the state's pueblos and reservations participate in the Pueblo Opera Program. POP, as the program is known, was established in 1973 and reaches more than 2,000 Native American children in New Mexico's 19 pueblos and on the Navajo and Apache reservations. Children and their families have supper on the opera grounds before attending a Youth Night performance.
- For information on the opera's annual family open house, please see our Event section.

SANTA FE PERFORMING ARTS SCHOOL & COMPANY
1050 Old Pecos Trail, 982-7992
www.sfperformingarts.org

Life's a Stage—Santa Fe has several theater companies that work with children and teens.
Photograph by James Black courtesy Santa Fe Performing Arts School & Company

This performing arts school and company, established in 1987, supports children and theater in Santa Fe. The school's mission is to give young people a vehicle for self-discovery and expression, to provide a well-rounded training in the performing arts disciplines and to reach out to the community, particularly children who otherwise would not be exposed to theater. SFPA's year around educational programming welcomes school-age children and teens. The company has attracted more than 10,000 students who have worked in more than 90 productions, entertaining more than 100,000 audience members.

The company offers after-school and summer classes in drama, music and dance for children ages 6-18. The City Different Players, an after-school performing arts program for 8-12 year olds, concludes their study with a full scale production at the end of each semester. These productions are open to the public and include special low cost weekday performances for elementary school classes to attend. The Teen Company is composed of 13-18 year olds who attend after-school and summer classes in drama, music and dance. Their program also culminates in productions open to the public.

The company's Artists-in-the-Schools Residency Program allows SFPA instructors to go into low-income public elementary schools and work with the classroom teachers to integrate performing arts into the curriculum. SFPA has a scholarship fund that provides financial assistance to children from low income families who would like to attend any of the programs.

SANTA FE PRO MUSICA
1405 Luisa Street, 988-4640 or 800-960-6680
www.santafepromusica.com

Since 1980 Santa Fe Pro Musica has offered a multi-faceted music education program for the young people of northern New Mexico. The company strives to meet the needs of a variety of students, from those who are attending a classical music event for the first time to those who plan a career in music. Santa Fe Pro Musica has a five point music outreach program: youth concerts, scholarship competition, free tickets, the musical instrument drive and the Apprentice String Quartet. Santa Fe Pro Musica is committed to keeping all these programs free for the students, their schools and their families.

The company usually offers five free youth concerts each season, from October through April. The concerts reach thousands of elementary school students in Santa Fe and northern New Mexico and are open to public and private schools as well as to home-school families. Age appropriate music education materials and music CDs are provided for each participating classroom or family and Spanish language translation of the materials is available. Santa Fe Pro Musica pays all expenses including student transportation.

Another ongoing student outreach project is the Santa Fe Pro Musica Young Artists Scholarship Competition. This program is designed for New Mexico resident musicians under the age of 19 who have advanced musical training and skills and wish to continue their music studies in college. A selected group of finalists perform at a live audition open to the public. In addition to a certificate and a cash prize, the competition winner(s) is given an opportunity to perform in a recital for the public.

The Santa Fe Pro Musica Apprentice String Quartet consists of four young musicians, two violinists, one violist, and one cellist, all under the age of 14. Under the guidance of Santa Fe Pro Musica guest artists and orchestra members, the String Quartet rehearses regularly throughout the season. The apprentices perform at social events and present a public performance at the end of the season. This program offers advanced young musicians the opportunity to be mentored by professional musicians, to learn rehearsal skills, team work, and performance techniques.

As a co-sponsor with the Rotary Clubs of Santa Fe, Pro Musica helps with a musical instrument drive. The Rotary Club refurbishes the instruments donated to Pro Musica and then gives them to the schools for use by children in band, violin, guitar, mariachi and general music classes.

SANTA FE SYMPHONY
551 West Cordova Road, Suite D, 983-1414
www.sf-symphony.org

The Santa Fe Symphony offers half-price tickets to children between the ages of 6 and 14, and a ten percent discount to older students. (Children under age 6 are not permitted at regular performances.) The symphony has an active outreach program of concerts in the schools and offers a no-cost children's performance annually for fourth graders at the Lensic Performing Arts Center. With the help of the Fanfare guild, the symphony provides vouchers for Santa Fe Public School's music teachers to attend Santa Fe Symphony concerts for free.

Other concerts for children have included:
- Four brass quintet performances at three local public elementary schools
- A 12-piece orchestra performance of Scott Joplin music at the Santa Fe Children's Museum
- Two full symphony orchestra performances of *Peter and the Wolf* with the narration in English and Spanish.

Symphony scholarships send as many as 40 selected young music students to the Santa Fe Public Schools Summer Band Camp at Capshaw Middle School for six weeks during the summer. Support and funding for children's programs comes from FanFare.

THE SANTA FE YOUTH SYMPHONY
1050 Old Pecos Trail (Armory for the Arts), 982-8483
www.sfys.org

The Santa Fe Youth Symphony Association, founded in 1994, brings music education to children ages 8 to 20. The group concentrates on instruments, especially strings, which are not stressed in music education in the schools. The program has mentored and offered scholarships to more than 1,500 students. Multi-level programs offered include the Youth Symphony, three string orchestras, a symphonic band, two jazz ensembles, the Ambassador Chamber Music Program, the Mozart y Mariachi Program (offered through elementary schools), the Endangered Instruments Program and the Chorus Program. Some young musicians participate in more than one.

The group's mission is to provide an opportunity for young musicians to develop and improve their musical skills in a quality musical environment, and to perform in public concerts in Santa Fe and northern New Mexico. All of the ensembles perform concerts in the public schools and at St. Francis Auditorium at the Museum of Fine Arts.

The organization uses older students as mentors for less experienced musicians and offers scholarships to qualifying students based on financial need.

All Santa Fe Youth Symphony concerts are free.

SITE SANTA FE
1606 Paseo de Peralta, 989-1199
www.sitesantafe.org

Young Curators—Site Santa Fe's programs for young people include the Young Curator's project which gives teens a chance to organize art shows. *Photograph courtesy Site Santa Fe*

SITE Santa Fe's Young Curators is a weekly after school and summer program for middle and high school students. The purpose of the program is to help teenagers connect with contemporary art and to allow them to explore the structure and production of exhibitions. The program encourages critical thinking about the role of art in our society in general and our community in particular. Participants create two shows each year comprised of art by their peers, other local, regional and national artists between the ages of 13 and 21.

The Young Curators learn the skills and procedures necessary for creating an exhibition. They determine the theme for the show, put out a call for entries, write curatorial statements, press releases and grants. They also choose the artwork and install the exhibition. The exhibitions are held in such venues such as the Museum of Fine Arts, Santa Fe, the Capitol Rotunda Gallery, the Santa Fe Art Institute and the Harwood Art Center in Albuquerque.

The Visual Thinking Strategies (VTS) program offers a way to introduce younger students to the world of art and, at the same time, exercise their critical thinking and communication skills. The program, operated through the Santa Fe Public schools as a school day or after school program, is for students in kindergarten through sixth grade. SITE Santa Fe provides busses, art-making materials and slides or posters and offers the VTS program in Spanish and in English.

SOUTHWEST CHILDREN'S THEATER PRODUCTIONS
142 East DeVargas Street, 984-3055
www.southwestchildrenstheatre.com

Southwest Children's Theater Productions is a non-profit organization that teaches theater to children and regularly stages children's plays. Established in 1988, SWCTP is the resident children's company of the Santa Fe Playhouse, Santa Fe's oldest community theater. The company offers productions of quality plays for and with children, an after-school program, summer theater classes and educational outreach programs that welcome children to the magic of performing live on stage.

SWCTP offers two after-school theater arts classes: the Budding Actor's Class for students in the first and second grades and the Young Actors Class for those in grades three through eighth. Both programs are held at the Santa Fe Playhouse. The main productions resulting from the classes feature classic fairy tales, folktales from around the world and original plays with music. Offered three times each year (spring, summer and fall), these shows bring professional actor adults and children together on stage for public performances held in a real theater—Santa Fe Playhouse.

The Summer Theatre program teaches children to create their own characters and plot for the Sizzlin' Summer Sensational Show, a production complete with original songs (they write the lyrics themselves, too) and music. That program also culminates with public performances.

WAREHOUSE 21
1614 Paseo de Peralta, 989-4423
www.warehouse21.org

An art and culture center for youth ages 12 to 21, Warehouse 21 offers year-round workshops in the performing, visual, media and literary arts as well as music and dance. Classes are either free or charge a modest fee. Ongoing special events produced by young people include theater, art and photography exhibitions, mural projects, youth concerts and more. W21, as the center is known, works on community service projects with young people referred by Teen Court and Municipal Court as well as high school students from throughout the city. Since 1997, W21 programs have served more than 25,000 teenagers and young adults from all socio-economic and cultural backgrounds.

W21's philosophy is characterized by a three-word slogan: "Do it yourself!" Young participants plan and produce their events and products to bring to local audiences. W21's Youth Video Forums feature teen video makers and original works. In partnership with KSFR, 90.7FM, Santa Fe's public access radio station, W21 teens produce the "Original Ground Zero" youth radio show. The center promotes local teen comedy and original theatrical pieces.

One of W21's most popular programs is Promoter's Circle, a collective of young people who book, promote, produce and help manage concerts for those under 21. Almost every weekend, W21 rocks with local and out of state touring bands. Other special events include poetry nights and video forums. W21 members publish Broad Issues, a youth "MagaZINE" featuring interviews, art, poetry, photography, stories and cartoons. The W21 silkscreen press studio is a popular place for printing t-shirts, patches and flyers.

GET MOVIN'

n introduction

There's a lot to do in Santa Fe, and that doesn't just mean going to museums. If you want to swim, learn karate, hike, ride a raft down a river, play tennis, ski or snowboard or ride a horse, you can do it here. The city has places to skateboard and trails for mountain biking. There's a municipal golf course as well as many places to play golf on nearby Indian land.

If you like to be outdoors, you're in luck here. The climate in Northern New Mexico is generally mild. The summer and fall months are characterized by daytime temperatures in the mid-80s and cool nights. Winters are also mild, but snow depths on the nearby mountains can average 8 to 10 feet. The rainy season normally begins mid-July and lasts until mid-September. Usually the rain is nothing more than a slight inconvenience, or even a welcome cooling off on a warm day.

If you'd like to hike with a group, the Santa Fe Sierra Club offers an ongoing program of weekend hikes and bird watching trips. You can learn more on their website, www.riogrande.sierra-club.org/santafe/outings.html The area has an assortment of hiking trails for all ability levels and the Sierra Club's guide to Santa Fe hikes, available in most Santa Fe book stores, is a good place to start your research.

One of the city's best kept secrets is the Santa Fe Ski Area, located just 20 miles from the Plaza. This family-run, family-friendly

Active Fun—Santa Fe has parks, playgrounds and nearby mountains for hiking and rivers for rafting. *Photograph courtesy New Mexico Department of Tourism*

ski hill offers classes for children in skiing and snowboarding and has a small childcare program.

Santa Fe's largest indoor recreation center, the Genoveva Chavez Community Center, is on the southside of town near Santa Fe Place mall. The city has fields for outdoor sports at the Municipal Recreation Complex and Marty Sanchez Links de Santa Fe west of town as well as Salvador Perez Park, Ragel Park and elsewhere. You'll find smaller parks throughout the city, including a few "passive" parks designed for enjoying the scenery rather than playing sports. The city's recreation centers offer a variety of classes, usually including martial arts for children. (Santa Fe also has a healthy assortment of private martial arts studios.)

If you want to join a team, you can choose from basketball, swimming, tennis, soccer, football, baseball and softball, volleyball and more. In addition to school-based teams, basketball is available through the Santa Fe Boys and Girls Club. Other sports are offered by the city and private organizations. If you'd like further information about youth sports teams, please call the City of Santa Fe Recreation Division, 955-2500.

(All area codes are 505 unless indicated otherwise.)

FISHING

Let's Fish—Not everyone is lucky enough to catch a brown trout, but fishing is still great!
Photograph by Marty Frentzel

SANTA FE NATIONAL FOREST/BUREAU OF LAND MANAGEMENT
1474 Rodeo Road, 438-7840
www.fs.fed.us/r3/sfe/recreation/fishing

NEW MEXICO DEPARTMENT OF GAME AND FISH
One Wildlife Way, 476-8000, (800) ASK-FISH (275-3474)
www.wildlife.state.nm.us/recreation/fishing/index.htm

Fishing is a great way to enjoy the forests, streams, rivers and lakes around Santa Fe. The Santa Fe National Forest has more than 620 miles of streams and lakes. Many of these are stocked with rainbow trout and the native cutthroat trout. Fishing licenses can be obtained at the New Mexico Game and Fish Department. Children younger than age 12 can fish for free in New Mexico, no license required. You'll find fishing streams and mountain lakes in the Santa Fe National Forest above Pecos, N.M. and in the Jemez mountains near Los Alamos.

Many Indian pueblos in the Santa Fe area open their land to public fishing, mostly for rainbow trout, some with bass or catfish. Tribal permits usually range from $5 to $15 a day for adults, often less for juniors and seniors.

If you want to learn to fly fish, Santa Fe has several shops that specialize in flies to tantalize the fish and other equipment. The staff members at these stores can suggest good spots to practice or recommend a guided fishing trip that includes lessons. If you prefer a lake, consider Cochiti Lake, Abiquiu Lake, Santa Cruz Lake or Monastery Lake, all an easy drive from Santa Fe.

The New Mexico Department of Game and Fish maintains a toll-free number for fishing information 24 hours a day: (800) ASK-FISH (275-3474). You can also find a report of fishing conditions on their website.

HIKE AND BIKE

RANDALL DAVEY AUDUBON CENTER
1800 Upper Canyon Rd., 983-4609
www.nm.audubon.org

SANTA FE NATIONAL FOREST/BUREAU OF LAND
MANAGEMENT
1474 Rodeo Road, 438-7840
www.fs.fed.us/r3/sfe/recreation/index.html

SIERRA CLUB NORTHERN NEW MEXICO GROUP
1472 S. St. Francis Dr., 983-2703
www.riogrande.sierraclub.org/santafe/Outings.html

You don't have to go far to find a trail or public pathway in Santa Fe and the surrounding area where you can walk, hike or ride a bike. In addition to in-town opportunities, the Santa Fe National Forest, just a few miles from downtown, offers longer, more strenuous hikes as well as gentle family trails. There are several places to rent mountain bikes in Santa Fe, and usually the staff at those stores can give you ideas on where to ride.

Here are a few suggestions for places to hike or mountain bike. There are many more opportunities to explore. Before you begin, remember that the altitude may take a little getting used to. Your heart and lungs work harder at 7,000 feet. Take it slowly and be sure to drink plenty of water.

For family hikes, a good place to start is the Randall Davey Audubon Center, at the end of Upper Canyon Road. This wildlife sanctuary, which is also the state office for the National Audubon Society, welcomes visitors year round. The center will give you a fine introduction to the plants and animals of the Santa Fe area. It encompasses 135 acres, bounded by thousands of acres of National Forest and Santa Fe River watershed. The center provides a safe habitat for plants and animals. Bird watchers have spotted approximately 130 species of birds here. Families are welcome on the regularly scheduled bird walks.

The property, the former site of a sawmill and, after that, the home of Santa Fe artist Randall Davey, has two hiking trails that meander into the piñon and juniper woodlands and climb up to a cool ponderosa pine forest. El Temporal is a half-mile loop. Bear Canyon offers a more challenging hike up a side canyon of the Santa Fe River Canyon—about a mile and a half before the walls become too steep to climb. If you walk quietly and keep on the lookout, you might catch a glimpse of a deer, bear or mountain lion, along with coyote, gray fox, bobcat, and long-tailed weasels.

The center's volunteers and staff can provide a trail guide, a list of birds you might see here and other information. The center also offers guided hikes and wildlife interpretive programs. Throughout the year, classes are held in a large indoor classroom and on the trails of the sanctuary. Adapted for different age groups, the classes encourage science investigation, nature exploration, creative arts, history, story telling, hiking and active play in the outdoors. In the summer, children flock to the Audubon Center for an eight-week summer camp filled with arts and crafts and outdoor activities with a focus on natural history. At the visitors center and nature store you'll find children's books and nature-related toys.

In the heart of town, the Santa Fe River Trail is an easy place for a stroll beneath big cottonwood trees. On the south side of town, the broad, paved Arroyo Chamisos Trail is a good bet for walkers and bikes and families with strollers. The well-used trail links several parks and connects with the longer Santa Fe Rail Trail. This trail begins as a level paved path running along the railroad tracks between Zia and Siringo roads and then heads out into the county as a dirt path and a popular route for mountain bikes.

Santa Fe's newest trail system, the Dale Ball Trails, opened for hiking and biking in 2001. The 31-miles of trails offer short loops, serious hikes and mountain bike single track rides. One trail head is about ten minutes from the Plaza off Hyde Park Road, also known as N.M. highway 475, at the intersection of Sierra del Norte. The other starting point is near the intersection of Cerro Gordo and Upper Canyon Road.

A popular, more strenuous hike, the Atalaya Trail, will take you to the top of Atalaya Mountain near St. John's College in Santa Fe's foothills. The summit is 9,121 feet and the view of Santa Fe worth the effort. The hike starts in the parking lot of St. John's College and involves some scrambling over rocks.

For an easier walk, try Lower Tesuque Creek, a relatively flat trail along a stream. This is a good family outing for spotting butterflies or lizards and splashing in the water. To reach the trail head, take Bishop's Lodge road approximately 4.5 miles from town to County Road 72A in Tesuque; turn right and look for signs for trailhead parking.

About 26 miles southwest of Santa Fe on State Road 14, the Cerrillos Hills Historic Park offers another outdoor experience. The park, half a mile north of the village of Cerrillos, has trails and open space for hiking, mountain biking and exploring. The trails here range from ¾ mile to a three-mile loop, and the views are memorable. You'll see signs of the busy mining area this landscape once was.

For another kind of hiking and biking trails, head out of town to the Santa Fe National Forest. The forest boundary lies just seven miles from downtown and opens into more than 300,000 acres of tree-studded land. The Santa Fe National Forest is one of the five national forests in New Mexico. The forest covers 1.6 million acres in the heart of north central New Mexico. Within the borders are lush meadows, miles of conifer trees, and a dormant volcano with a 15-mile wide crater (Valles Caldera National Preserve). Elevations rise from 5,300 to 13,103 feet at the summit of Truchas Peak, located within the Pecos Wilderness.

Take a Hike—Among the many places to discover near Santa Fe is Aspen Vista in the Santa Fe National Forest. *Photograph by Don Strel*

Visitors can enjoy camping, fishing, hiking and many other outdoor recreation activities. The Santa Fe National Forest is administered though a Forest Supervisor's Office and five ranger districts. There are 1,002 miles of trails, some maintained by volunteer groups. Many summer hiking trails become cross-country ski and snowmobile trails in winter. There are 291,669 acres of wilderness in the Santa Fe National Forest. Travel here is restricted to foot or horseback. Wilderness areas include Pecos, San Pedro Parks, Dome and the Chama River Canyon.

Convenient to Santa Fe, the Borrego Trail offers a pleasant stroll. This hike is a loop with some uphill into an aspen-fir forest. To reach the trail head, take Hyde Park Road for eight miles. After passing the Hyde State Park sign, turn immediately into the paved parking lot on your left. Beginning at the parking lot, the trail drops down into a lovely shady valley full of flowers during the summer. The trail continues, climbing onto a ridge and dropping down to Tesuque Creek, where a fallen log makes a handy bridge. The Borrego route was once a way to bring sheep from the northern villages into Santa Fe.

The Black Canyon Trail is a short, easy loop through an aspen and fir forest, a good hike for younger children. The first half-mile of this loop trail goes through the Black Canyon Campground, then gently rises through a grove of aspen and evergreens, opening to offer mountain views. To find the trail from Santa Fe, drive to the Black Canyon campground seven miles up Hyde Park Road. Please park outside the fence; parking inside the campground is reserved for paying campers.

The Santa Fe Ski Area, at the end of Hyde Park Road, 15 miles from downtown, is a great place for hiking, biking and exploring during summer and early fall. Wildflowers and butterflies are abundant. There's a stream to jump across as you wander up the beginner's ski slope. You may see chipmunks, squirrels, marmots, colorful mushrooms and butterflies. An aspen viewing chairlift ride is often available in the fall, and you can hike down the ski slope from the unloading area at the top of Tesuque Peak.

Need more suggestions? The Sierra Club of Santa Fe has put together a hiking guide, *Day Hikes in the Santa Fe Area*, available at many book stores, which offers a fine listing of trails and their difficulty rating. The club also offers weekly hikes with a guide.

HORSEBACK RIDING

The Santa Fe area offers many places to ride and several locations to rent horses. As you'd expect, most of the stables are a little ways out of town. All commercial stables have gentle horses for beginners. Some of the rides will explore sandy arroyos and rolling hills. Others head for higher landscapes dotted with pine trees, mountain streams and summer wild flowers. Rides are available by the hour, half day and at sunset. Many stables also offer lessons. For one- to three-hour tours, be ready to spend $50 or more. Each outfitter has different limits as to age and weight, so call ahead. You won't need boots, but be sure to wear shoes that protect your toes and long pants for a more comfortable ride. Many outfitters prohibit shorts and sandals for your own protection. If you wear a hat make sure it fits so that it will not fall off while you're on the trail.

Please check online, in the phone book or with the Santa Fe Convention and Visitors Bureau for specific information about where to rent horse and take riding lessons.

PUBLIC PARKS AND PLAYGROUNDS

Rolling Along—Don't overlook Santa Fe's public parks, playgrounds and bike paths for outdoor fun. *Photograph courtesy New Mexico Department of Tourism*

Twice a year, the City of Santa Fe publishes a handy guide to city recreation facilities. You'll find it at all city recreation centers, at the recreation office, 1142 Siler Road, or at City Hall, 200 Lincoln Ave. Here's a brief guide to city programs and facilities.

CITY OF SANTA FE SUMMER YOUTH RECREATION PROGRAMS
Santa Fe Community Services, 955-6568

The city uses many of its parks to offer summer programs for children ages 6-12 and for teens, ages 13-19. Both programs are inexpensive or free and run from mid-June through early August from 7:30 a.m. until 5:30 p.m. They are ideal for children with parents who don't get summer off! Program activities include team and individual sports, games, drama, arts and crafts, swimming, storytelling, field trips, computer classes and dance. Registration is held one day in mid-May on a first-come, first-served basis. The city also offers a series of special summer programs for kids and teens in swimming, golf, tennis, archery, gymnastics and cheerleading.

GENOVEVA CHAVEZ COMMUNITY CENTER
3221 Rodeo Rd., 955-4000
www.chavezcenter.org

Completed in 2000, this $25 million facility, the city's largest, welcomes more than 380,000 visitors each year. The center includes four major focuses: a fitness area, gymnasium, ice arena and swimming pools. Here you'll find Santa Fe's only full-sized indoor ice skating rink, open year round, with skate rentals, a youth hockey program and learn-to-skate classes. The center has a 50-meter lap pool, a therapy pool and a leisure pool with three diving boards. Older kids love the two-story waterslide, whirlpools and the river. Little ones can splash in the toddler area and play on the frog slide. The center offers swimming lessons, scuba and snorkeling classes and a beginning kayak program.

The Chavez Center also has an indoor running track, a full gymnasium for basketball and volleyball and racquetball courts. You'll find summer recreation programs, after-school programs and camps for kids during winter and spring breaks. Teens are encouraged to use the center's workout facility with weights, cardio machines and fitness classes of all sorts. The center's PlayZone provides child care for ages 2 through 6 while the parents exercise.

FORT MARCY COMPLEX
490 Washington Avenue, 955-2500

Just a short walk from the Plaza, this recreation complex features both indoor and outdoor possibilities. Inside, you'll find a tot pool and lap pool, a gymnasium usually alive with basketball games, a weight room, racquetball courts and a fitness room occupied with classes for children and adults. Students age 13 and older may use the weight room, gym and racquetball courts.

The outdoor fields welcome baseball and soccer players. There's also a paved walking or jogging track. Fort Marcy hosts special events, including sports tournaments for kids and adults during the year. Other programs include the cheer and drill clinic for girls in grades 4-7, a summer youth sports camp and girls' volleyball clinic.

SALVADOR PEREZ PARK
601 Alta Vista Street, 955-2604

This neighborhood park, a popular spot with soccer teams and Little League, offers sports fields and an indoor pool and weight room open to teens and adults. There are also tennis courts and two separate play lots for kids including one especially designed for pre-schoolers.

BICENTENNIAL POOL AND PARK
1121 Alto Street, 955-4779

Santa Fe's only public outdoor pool, the Bicentennial has a fenced wading pool, complete with frog slide and mushroom waterfall for the little guys. The larger pool has time set aside for laps as well as family recreational fun. The adjoining park has equipment well-suited for young kids and also offers tennis courts and basketball areas. Baseball fields are nearby.

MUNICIPAL RECREATION COMPLEX AND MARTY SANCHEZ LINKS DE SANTA FE
205 Caja del Río (west of city) 955-4400.

The big attraction here is 27 holes of golf set in the rolling hills outside Santa Fe with expansive views of the surrounding mountains. The complex offers golf lessons, a putting green and driving range. A golf shop and restaurant overlooking part of the fairway add to its appeal. For non-golfers, the complex has sand volleyball courts, fields for youth rugby, a youth BMX park and soccer fields.

OTHER CITY PARKS OF INTEREST:

ATALAYA
717 Camino Cabra, (next to Atalaya Elementary School)

Along with stunning views of Atalaya Mountain, this quiet park features a long metal slide embedded into the hillside, swings, picnic tables, tennis and basketball courts.

RAGLE PARK
Zia and Yucca Roads

This popular park, located in a child-filled neighborhood, has a small playground with equipment including slides, a fire pole and tunnels, all enclosed by a fence. Adjacent ball fields are used for soccer, baseball games and free play. This busy place sits just off the Arroyo Chamisos trail. It's a good place to play before and after a family walk or jog.

FRANKLIN MILES PARK
1027 Camino Carlos Rey (at Siringo Road)

This large park has sports playing fields, a playground, basketball courts and grassy picnic areas, which are a rarity in Santa Fe. It's the site of one of the city's two skate parks where kids are encouraged to ride and try tricks on their skateboards and BMX bikes.

VILLA LINDA PARK
4250 Cerrillos Road (near Santa Fe Place mall)

Location is the main attraction here. This small park offers toddlers and children a playground and room for fun before or after a shopping trip.

DE VARGAS SKATEBOARD PARK
302 West DeVargas

This small downtown park along the Santa Fe River is best known for its skateboard ramps. It's walking distance from the Plaza. The park also has picnic tables.

RANDALL DAVEY AUDUBON CENTER
1800 Upper Canyon Road, 983-4609
www.nm.audubon.org

The Randall Davey Audubon Center encompasses 135 acres, bounded by thousands of acres of National Forest and Santa Fe River watershed land. The Center provides safe habitat for plants and animals. Bird watchers have spotted approximately 130 species of birds here.

The Audubon Society acquired this property, the former site of a sawmill and after that, the home of Santa Fe artist Randall Davey, in the mid-1980s. Operated as a nature center, it offers two hiking trails that meander into the piñon and juniper woodlands and climb up to a cool ponderosa pine forest. The center's volunteers and staff can provide a trail guide, a list of birds you might see here and other information. The center also offers guided hikes, wildlife interpretive programs and summer activities for children. At the visitors center and nature store you'll find children's books and nature-related toys

The Audubon Center has two major trails: El Temporal and Bear Canyon. El Temporal is a half-mile loop. After a short initial climb, the trail is relatively level throughout. Bear Canyon offers a more challenging hike up a side canyon of the Santa Fe River Canyon—about a mile and a half before the walls become too steep to climb. If you walk quietly and keep on the lookout, aside from the numerous species of birds, you just might catch a glimpse of a deer, bear or mountain lion, along with coyote, gray fox, bobcat, and long-tailed weasels.

RIVER RAFTING

If you like wet and wild excitement, take a river trip. Discover the Rio Grande, the largest river in New Mexico, from inside a big rubber raft. Raft trips offered by commercial companies in Santa Fe or Taos include adventures suitable for children and adults. Many trips on the Rio Grande, parts of which are classified as a Wild and Scenic River, take you through a 50-mile stone gorge, a rift in the crust of several ancient lava flows. You'll find the biggest rapids on the Taos Box trips, generally recommended for people age 12 and older. The rapids on the lower section of the river, known as The Racecourse, are suitable for younger children. Scenic float trips are also available.

You can usually take a trip from the early spring until mid-summer, and spend half or a full day on the river. Availability of raft trips depends on the previous winter's snow depth and the summer rainfall, but the rafting season usually starts in mid or late May when the melting snow gives the Rio Grande sufficient water. You might be able to raft into mid August depending on our summer rains. The Rio Grande depths vary according to location. In some spots the river is shallow and can be measured in inches; other parts are more than twenty feet deep.

The Rio Chama, the major tributary of the Rio Grande, enters the state atop Cumbres Pass north of Chama. In a wet year, this is another place for great rafting. The most popular stretch of the Chama, with a Wild and Scenic River designation, is the 33 miles between El Vado and Abiquiu reservoirs. This section is open to rafters during seven summer weekends. Twelve outfitters offer guided trips, mostly overnight, through this stretch of water. It's about a 100 mile drive from Santa Fe to El Vado.

If you take a raft trip, no matter what time of year, be prepared to get wet! The raft companies all provide life vests and will remind you to wear plenty of sunscreen. To find companies that offer trips, look online, in the phone book, ask the Santa Fe Chamber of Commerce or inquire at a sporting goods store. The state of New Mexico has more information about rafting on its website: www.newmexico.org/go/loc/outdoors/page/recreation-boating-rafting.html

WINTER SPORTS

Winter Wonderful—Santa Fe and Northern New Mexico offer abundant opportunities to snowboard, ski and enjoy winter. *Photograph by Michael Darter courtesy Ski Santa Fe*

ANGEL FIRE RESORT
Angel Fire, N.M. (90 miles north of Santa Fe), 377-4316
www.angelfireresort.com

ENCHANTED FOREST
3 miles east of Red River, N.M., 754-2374 or 1-800-966-9381
www.enchantedforestxc.com

PAJARITO MOUNTAIN SKI AREA
397 Camp May Road, Los Alamos N.M. (Off NM 501 north of Los Alamos), 662-5725
www.skipajarito.com

SKI SANTA FE
16 miles northeast of Santa Fe on highway 475 (Artist Road/Hyde Park Road), 982-4429
(Chipmunk Corner 988-9636 for daycare reservations)
www.skisantafe.com

TAOS SKI VALLEY
72 miles north of Santa Fe off NM 522, 866-968-7386
www.skitaos.org

VALLES CALDERA NATIONAL PRESERVE
Office: 2201 Trinity Drive
Los Alamos, 661-3333
www.vallescaldera.gov

For downhill skiing and snowboarding convenience, you can't beat Ski Santa Fe. Only 16 miles from the Plaza, the area offers Santa Fe's winter visitors access to slopes for skiing and snowboarding. The family-owned establishment provides a safe place for pre-schoolers to learn to ski, a ski school program especially for children, and an easy-to-ride beginner lift. Ski Santa Fe, in the Sangre de Cristo mountain range, is northeast of town in the Santa Fe National Forest.

In addition to its beginner friendly slopes, the ski area has plenty of challenging terrain, too. The 12,053-foot summit is the highest in New Mexico. The area offers 44 runs ranging from smooth, easy trails to tough shoots winding through the trees. There are six lifts with plans for a seventh to be installed over the summer of 2005. Chipmunk Corner provides a nursery and daycare for children from 3 months to 3 years (reservations needed) and supervised snow play for children up to 4 years old. For older kids, Ski Santa Fe offers ski and snowboard lessons and plenty of room to practice what you've learned. For better learning, enrollment is limited in all children's programs. Full day packages include lessons, equipment rentals if needed, and lunch.

In addition to Ski Santa Fe, the Taos Ski Valley and Pajarito Mountain near Los Alamos are close enough to Santa Fe to provide a family day trip. Each offers lessons just for children and equipment rentals. (No snowboards are allowed at Taos.) Angel Fire Resort, about 90 miles north from Santa Fe, is especially family friendly. With two high-speed quads, four freestyle terrain parks, a halfpipe and areas for snowmobiling, tubing, ice skating and cross-country skiing, the resort caters to a wide range of ages and interests. In addition to skiing and snowboarding, the area has a tubing/sledding area (with rentals available) that is open daily until 9 p.m. (evenings under lights). The tubing hill even has a moving carpet, similar to a conveyor belt, to bring you back to the top for another slide down. The ski resort also offers snowshoeing and sleigh rides.

CROSS-COUNTRY SKIING, SLEDDING, TUBING AND SNOWSHOEING

Children Welcome—Ski Santa Fe and other northern New Mexico ski areas offer special classes for children who want to learn to ski.
Photograph by Michael Darter courtesy Ski Santa Fe

Cross-country skiing is a popular sport for New Mexico families, with many options for trails, beginning with the closest untraveled dirt road after a good snow storm. If you're a beginner, look for cross country ski lessons often available through Santa Fe Community College or advertised in area sporting goods stores which also rent the necessary equipment. The same mountain and foothill trails that make good hiking can be used for snowshoeing and cross country skiing.

The NORSKI Track Ski Trail offers an opportunity for track skiing close to Santa Fe. You'll find the trail a quarter mile before the Santa Fe Ski Basin, and just east of Vista Grande parking area off Hyde Park Road/State Highway 475. The trail is 2.4 miles. Constructed, maintained and operated by the NORSKI Racing Club, this one-way trail includes terrain for beginners and advanced skiers with cross-overs so that younger children do not have to finish the entire course. And the mountain scenery is beautiful!

One of the most popular spots for family winter outings is Black Canyon. The three-mile round trip trail has good views and a variety of terrain that most cross country beginners can handle. Park outside the Black Canyon Campground, which is closed in the winter. The trail begins seven miles from town, up Hyde Park Road/State Road 475.

Farther up the road in the Santa Fe National Forest is the Aspen Vista/Tesuque Peak Road, another great place for cross country skiing or snowshoe trips. The wide road, which is closed to motorized vehicles including snowmobiles, presents a gradual uphill climb. You can access this trail from Aspen Vista Picnic Area, just beyond the 13 mile marker, 13 miles up Hyde Park Road/State Road 475.

The Valles Caldera west of Los Alamos in the Jemez Mountains is another spot with fine cross country skiing terrain. Skiing is permitted on Fridays, Saturdays and Sundays. No advance reservations are required, but you need to purchase a day pass at the welcome area, located two miles from the main entrance. The gate is at mile marker 392 on State Road 4.

If you have a full day or more, you may want to visit Enchanted Forest, a 600-acre cross-country center near Red River in northeastern New Mexico. The area offers tracks, trails through the trees, equipment rental, instruction and more. Enchanted Forest is New Mexico's largest full-service cross country ski area offering trails groomed for both classic and freestyle skiing. The facility, 3 miles east of Red River in the Carson National Forest, has gorgeous mountain vistas and meandering forest trails which give a back country feel in a groomed, patrolled area. The trail system is groomed with one side tracked for classic or diagonal stride skiing and the other left smooth for snowshoeing and freestyle or skate skiing.

Enchanted Forest has beginner, intermediate and advanced lessons, including classic and skating techniques. The ski area has two warming huts and trail-side picnic areas. The Enchanted Forest also offers over 15km of exclusive snowshoeing trails. It's a long ride from Red River to Santa Fe—more than a hundred miles. You may want to consider spending the night there.

If you like winter in the mountains, Hyde Park and the Santa Fe National Forest offer plenty of beautiful places for building a snowman or sledding and tubing. One popular place is just up the hill from the Black Canyon Campground mentioned earlier in this section. Another good spot is the Big Tesuque, two or three miles up Hyde Park Road/State Road 475 from Black Canyon.

Closer to town, several city parks become winter wonderlands with the addition of fresh snow. The Patrick Smith Park, just off Canyon Road, has some nice hills for sleds and tubes. (No sled or tube rentals are generally available in Santa Fe.)

Finally, be sure to check the weather before setting out for your winter fun. Remember that Santa Fe sits at 7,000 feet; weather conditions can change rapidly at this altitude. And, even though it's winter, don't forget the sunscreen.

KIDS' CLUBS AND PROGRAMS

An introduction

Santa Fe's attractions for children include the opportunity to get together with other kids, whether it's on the sports field or through an arts and crafts project. We've tried to mention some of the long-established programs for children in this section; the list is not complete but offers an overview. The City of Santa Fe Recreation Department, 955-2100, is a fine resource for people looking for child-friendly sports programs or multi-purpose clubs where kids and teens can have fun.

Looking for dance classes or drumming sessions outside the club environment? You'll find arts-related programs in our Arts section.

(All area codes are 505 unless indicated otherwise.)

Team work—Involvement in group activities, like building a bird house, helps kids learn to work together while they have fun. *Photograph courtesy Girls Inc.*

BIG BROTHERS BIG SISTERS OF SANTA FE
1225 St. Francis Drive, Suite B, 983-8360
www.bbbsofsantafe.org

Big Brothers Big Sisters of Santa Fe offers children ages 6–18 from single-parent families an adult mentor to provide extra attention and TLC. The child and the adult, known as the "Big," create their own activities and may participate in special events organized by BBBS. The adults are screened and offered professional support for this one-on-one mentoring. The Santa Fe program is part of the national organization, Big Brothers Big Sisters of America, and one of about 500 affiliates nationwide. BBBS of Santa Fe has been serving children in the Santa Fe community for more than 25 years.

BOY SCOUTS OF AMERICA, Great Southwest Council
5841 Office Boulevard NE, Albuquerque
(800) 368-9218 or 983-3488 in Santa Fe
www.gswcbsa.org

The Great Southwest Council, Boy Scouts of America field office is located in Santa Fe. Cub Scouting is for boys in first through fifth grade. Boy Scouts is for young men between the ages of 11 and 18. The scouting program also offers a young adult program for men and woman between the ages of 14 years and 21 years of age. This program, called Venturing, enables young people to participate in high adventure activities such as rock climbing, white water events and mountain biking. About 800 young people are involved in the Santa Fe programs. Interested children and young people are welcome to join scouting at any point in their lives. Adult volunteers are also needed.

The Cub Scouts are invited to an annual summer camp held in Santa Fe in June. The camp helps the scouts learn first aid skills, how to use bows and arrows, learn about nature and enjoy outdoor experiences.

The purpose of the Boy Scouts of America is to provide an effective program which will build desirable character, train young people to become participating citizens and develop personal fitness.

GIRLS INCORPORATED OF SANTA FE
301 Hillside Ave., 982-2042
www.girlsincofsantafe.org

Long Time Haven—Girls Inc. offers after school, summer and school break programs.
Photograph courtesy Girls Inc.

Girls Incorporated of Santa Fe, formerly known as the Santa Fe Girls Club, has been serving girls from kindergarten through middle school at the same location since 1957. In 1991, the club affiliated with Girls Incorporated, a national nonprofit youth organization dedicated to providing vital, innovative educational programs to girls, particularly those who are underserved or at risk. The programs are researched, developed and evaluated nationally for effectiveness and implemented by a trained staff.

In Santa Fe, "After School at Hillside" provides every girl with programs designed to inspire her to be strong, smart, and bold! Sports, arts, cooking, science, homework help, field trips and more are included in the curriculum. The club has a free van which picks up girls from many Santa Fe schools and brings them to the downtown club. The van runs Monday through Friday until 6 p.m. Girls can participate full or part time and a sliding fee scale is available.

In addition to after school programs, the club offers day camps with indoor and outdoor activities. The schedule includes a 10-week summer camp, winter holiday camp and spring break camp which operates when schools are closed.

GIRL SCOUTS SANGRE DE CRISTO COUNCIL
450 St. Michael's Dr., 983-6339, 1-877-983-6339 (TOLL-FREE)
www.girlscouts-sdc.org

The Girl Scouts Sangre de Cristo Council provides activities to help girls learn and practice the skills they need to succeed in today's world. Through activities that build self-confidence, responsibility, integrity, creative decision-making skills and teamwork, the girls develop leadership abilities intended to last them a lifetime.

The Santa Fe Girl Scout program is open to any girl from age 5 to 17 and also welcomes adult volunteers. Programs are girl-driven, reflecting the ever-changing needs and interests of participating girls. Activities, which include community service projects, arts and crafts and outdoor explorations, encourage girls to discover and appreciate diversity. Girl Scouting helps girls develop concern for the well-being of their communities, promotes their understanding of how the quality of community life affects every member of society and encourages girls to use their skills to work with others for the benefit of all.

Girl Scout activities are designed to be age appropriate, with the girls of each troop having a strong voice in what they'd like to do. The youngest scouts, The Daisy Group, begin in kindergarten. The program serves girls of all ages with the Brownie, Junior, Cadette and Senior, for high school students.

The Sangre de Cristo Council raises money each year with the annual Great Cookie Caper, a competition which invites Santa Fe area chefs to create beautiful, great tasting desserts. The event encourages the public to vote for their favorite creation, and includes a silent auction.

Each summer, Camp Elliott Barker is the Sangre de Cristo Girl Scouts home away from home. This rustic retreat for girls ages 7 to 17 has been the destination for girls from all over northern New Mexico for more than 40 years. The resident camp is open to all girls interested in a creative outdoor experience. The campsite encompasses over 500 acres in the scenic Sangre de Cristo Mountains just outside Angel Fire, N.M. Horseback riding, archery, cookouts and arts and crafts are among the programs offered. Girls take part in activities that promote self-esteem, teamwork and an appreciation for the environment that encourages self-discovery and personal growth. Camp sessions run for four, six or ten days with special weekend programs for troops and families. The cost of camp is kept affordable and scholarships are available.

KIDS STUFF AND KIDS CAMPS
Santa Fe Community College, 6401 Richards Ave., 428-1676
www.sfccnm.edu/sfcc/pages/670.html

Santa Fe Community College isn't just for grown-ups. Through its Continuing Education program, the college offers a variety of opportunities for children, ages 5 to 13, to learn, have a good time and find out what it's like to be on a college campus. Classes for kids blend fun with education in a menu of classes that changes each semester. Topics often include guitar, tennis, swimming, clay and other arts and crafts, rock climbing, photographgraphy, woodturning, Spanish, babysitting, cooking, computers, hiking and sewing. Classes can continue in a series for several weeks, or may run for only one Saturday.

SFCC regularly offers spring break and summer camps for kids. Although the topics may change, summer camps usually focus on outdoor skills including high ropes, orienteering and zip lines and are offered for ages 8 to 13.

High school students are welcomed on campus with the Make Your Mark program, which reserves a select number of places in selected college art classes just for them.

MONICA ROYBAL CENTER
737 Agua Fría Street, ages 6-12, 955-6750; teen center, 955-6860
www.santafenm.gov/community-services/community-development/MonicaRoybalCenter.asp

Operated by the City of Santa Fe, the Monica Roybal Center provides recreational and educational programs for school-age children and youth. The center operates year-round, offering an after-school program during fall and spring as well as a full day summer recreation program. A variety of programs at the center help children develop self-esteem and leadership skills through support groups, workshops and cooperative interaction. The children develop their social skills by working together and improve motor skills when participating in the various activities. The center's goal is to reduce negative behavior and develop their members into positive role models in our community.

Designed for ages 13 to 19, the Monica Roybal Teen Center provides constructive, educational activities and a space for teenagers to socialize. The Teen Center offers many special events for teens including dances and field trips.

The summer program offers passive and active recreational, instructional and educational programs such as tennis, golf, gymnastics and archery for school age kids Monday through Friday from 7:30 a.m. to 5:30 p.m. Participating children also receive a free lunch and snacks at nine program sites throughout the city.

SANTA FE BOYS & GIRLS CLUBS
730 Alto Street and other locations, 983-6632
www.santafebgc.org

Since the program's inception in 1938, the Santa Fe Boys & Girls Clubs have provided activities and mentoring that promote the development of young people by instilling a sense of competence, usefulness and belonging. The organization was the first to offer safe, organized after school activities to Santa Fe youngsters. One goal of the club is to show kids and young people that they can and do make a difference in the world.

The Boys & Girls Clubs work with children and teens ages 6 through 18. Although the comprehensive programs, held after school, during school vacations and throughout the summer, are designed specifically for disadvantaged youth, the club is open to every child in Santa Fe County. The activities include a wide range of arts, sports and recreation. The Clubs have five locations throughout Santa Fe County: the original club on Alto Street and the expansions at Camino de Jacobo, Valle Vista, Santa Cruz and in Chimayo. The club buildings are located in areas where they can best serve low-income children. Three of the clubs are in housing projects to provide after school programming to youths where they live.

In addition to the overall program, the clubs also have specific activities designed for teens and for girls and offer computer technology classes. In addition to the free programs, the clubs also provide nutritional meals free to all participants. The clubs make free transportation available from school to the clubs sites for after school programs.

SANTA FE COUNTY 4-H
3229 Rodeo Road, 471-4711
http://.spectre.nmsu.edu/county/4h
(NOTE: this has to have the "http")

County-wide Opportunity—Santa Fe County 4-H operates in several communities with programs for children and teens. *Photograph courtesy Santa Fe County 4-H*

Santa Fe County has 14 4-H clubs with approximately 250 registered members. Each club meets at a different time and location to accommodate the needs of its communities.

The 4-H program provides children between the ages of 5 and 19 opportunities to learn life skills and gain knowledge while having fun. Five to 8 year-olds can join Cloverbuds, an exploratory non-competitive program for beginning 4-H'ers. Nine to 19 year-olds may participate in 4-H through community clubs, after-school programs, and classrooms.

The program encourages children to make contributions in areas such as environmental education, community service and current youth issues. 4-H offers more than 100 projects for children and teens to choose from, with choices ranging from leadership and communication to agriculture and home economics as well as engineering or woodworking. In addition to raising animals and growing plants, 4-H offers projects in creative arts, health and nutrition, natural science, communications and many more areas. Adults and youth spend time together learning new skills, developing hidden talents and making new friends. Santa Fe County 4-H welcomes adults to help with flexible short-term and long-term volunteer opportunities.

Santa Fe County 4-H is the youth development program of the Cooperative Extension Service, College of Agriculture and Home Economics, New Mexico State University.

SPECIAL OLYMPICS OF NEW MEXICO AREA 2
P.O. Box 1095, Santa Fe,
Director Janet Escudero, 982-2275

This all-volunteer program offers year-round sports training and athletic completions in a variety of Olympic-type sports for individuals with mental retardation. The program works with children and adults to give them continuing opportunities to develop physical fitness, demonstrate courage, experience joy and participate in sharing their own gifts, skills and friendships with their families, other Special Olympic athletes and the community.

The Santa Fe program is one of eight local programs in Northern New Mexico serving 350 athletes who work with 40 certified coaches. The area meets include athletics, softball, aquatics, cycling, bowling and golf. Athletes age 8 and older are eligible for the program. They receive eight weeks of training for each sport. Competitions are structured so athletes compete against others of similar ability. There is no cost to train or compete locally.

The program welcomes and trains volunteers for a variety of tasks including fundraising, coaching, paperwork and other jobs.

SPORTS AND ORGANIZED RECREATION

Team Sports—Kids can play baseball, soccer, football, tennis, hockey and many other sports. *Photograph courtesy Girls Inc.*

Santa Fe has all the expected team sports for children, plus some you might not expect, like youth hockey. The City of Santa Fe Recreation Department at 995-2500 is good place to begin your quest for information.

Here are some additional resources:

Baseball: For the Metro League, ages 5-12, call Erika Cummings, 476-9603. For the American League, call 299-1097. For the American Amateur Baseball Congress, Adrian Martinez, 988-7625.

Football: Santa Fe Children's Football League, ages 6-13, Eddie Webb, 989-4593; Young America Football League, 820-0775

Soccer: Northern New Mexico Soccer Club, ages 5–14 982-0878.

Basketball: Youth Basketball, Santa Fe Boys and Girls Club, 983-6632. Santa Fe Independent Youth Basketball, Tony Chavez, 4660-7543.

Hockey: Santa Fe Youth Hockey Association, Melissa Peterson, 986-1851

Fencing: New Mexico Fencing Foundation, 699-2034

DAY TRIPS

n introduction

In this chapter you'll learn about places to visit outside of Santa Fe. New Mexico is filled with wonderful places to go and things to see including Indian ruins, national parks, historic sights and outdoor experiences. We've only listed a few of them here. You can learn more about New Mexico at the state Visitor Information Center, across from the State Capitol at 491 Old Santa Fe Trail. You'll find maps, brochures about attractions in all parts of New Mexico and helpful staff members.

We've divided these attractions into three categories: Albuquerque, Los Alamos and Elsewhere. Not only is Albuquerque a big city with shopping malls, all the popular chain restaurants and lots of movie theaters, it offers quite a few attractions that make the trip worthwhile and fun, including the zoo, aquarium and botanic gardens.

In addition, we've included some of our other favorite spots outside of Santa Fe that are certainly worth a visit. All are close enough that you can come back to Santa Fe to spend the night.

(All area codes are 505 unless indicated otherwise. If admission is free, or discounts are offered for children, we noted it.)

Cheetahs and More—The Rio Grande Zoo is one of many attractions for children in Albuquerque. *Photo by Morys Hines courtesy of the Albuquerque Biological Park.*

DAY TRIPS: ALBUQUERQUE

THE ALBUQUERQUE AQUARIUM
2601 Central Ave. NW, Albuquerque, 764-6200
www.cabq.gov/biopark/aquarium/
Free for children under 3

Sharks Aplenty—The Albuquerque Aquarium offers all sorts of attractions for children and parents, including eels and sharks.
Photo by Ray Watt courtesy of the Albuquerque Biological Park

What a surprise to find an aquarium so far from an ocean! The Albuquerque Aquarium exhibits Gulf of Mexico saltwater species from a variety of habitats, including coral reefs, open ocean and deep ocean. In the 285,000-gallon ocean tank you can watch brown, sandtiger, blacktip and nurse sharks swimming alongside brilliantly colored reef fish, eels and sea turtles. The aquarium includes a jelly fish display, seahorses and other odd-looking ocean creatures. Don't miss the moray eels in their own mysterious eel cave.

The aquarium offers a hands-welcome touch pool exhibit where you can handle star fish and other water animals. The Ship's Cove features scale models of several historical sailing ships and three of more recent design. This area displays a mermaid figurehead, masts and sails, buoys, a ship's bell, lobster traps and maps. You can take charge of the interactive ship's wheel and you might find volunteers in the recreated ship's cabin demonstrating the art of model boat building.

The aquarium has two exhibits designed to teach you about waterlife in New Mexico. The first, called Rio Grande at Central Bridge, not only gives visitors a glimpse at the fish in the Rio Grande as it flows through modern Albuquerque, but also presents an idea of the life the river supported 100 years ago. The other, Rio Grande Cutthroat Trout Stream, lets visitors see a freshwater stream like those in northern New Mexico with the swiftly flowing, crystal clear, ice-cold water that native cutthroat trout require. Fallen logs and living trees add to the mountain stream ambience.

Expect to spend at least an hour here. You can grab lunch or a snack at the Aquarium's Shark Reef Café and watch fish swim as you relax.

Because the Aquarium is part of the Albuquerque BioPark, which also includes the Botanic Garden (which is on the same site as the aquarium) and the zoo, you can save money with a combination ticket. Children under 3 are free.

THE ALBUQUERQUE MUSEUM OF ART & HISTORY
2000 Mountain Road NW, Old Town, Albuquerque 242-4600, 243-7255
www.cabq.gov/museum
Children 3 and younger free

The Albuquerque Museum is dedicated to art, history and education. At its current location since 1979, and renovated and expanded in 2005, the museum has featured art of the Southwest, 400 years of Albuquerque history, educational classes and world-class traveling exhibitions.

The permanent history exhibit, Four Centuries: The History of Albuquerque, focuses on maps of the Southwestern United States, Spanish occupation and *El Camino Real*, the famous trade route from Mexico. Hispanic life, Civil War and New Mexico's journey to statehood in 1912 are also featured extensively. The museum's history collection includes arms and armor, Hispanic crafts, Victorian and decorative arts, maps and textiles.

The museum also has a nicely stocked gift shop.

EXPLORA!
1701 Mountain Road NW, Albuquerque, 224-8300
www.explora.mus.nm.us/index.htm

Discounted tickets for children ages 1-11. Under 1 year-old free. All children and toddlers must be accompanied by a paying adult.

This well designed science center features 250 interactive exhibits in many branches of science, technology and art to help children and adults unleash their brainpower. Explora! encompasses 50,000 square feet divided into cozy nooks and crannies for exploration and fun. It's just across the street from the New Mexico Museum of Natural History.

Explora! offers 50,000 square feet of ideas you can touch, a place where visitors are encouraged to keep their hands ON the exhibits. You'll find areas where you can experiment with water, wind power and electricity. Don't miss the enclosed Ball Run and make-your-own-ball-run area, the experiment bar, art project areas and the high-wire bike. A robot lab, the Paradox Café with brain teasers on the menu and giant bubble equipment are all part of the fun.

Explora! has a special place for toddlers and opens early on Mondays for children 4 and younger. The large staff of helpful folks makes your experience here even more fun. The center is a private, nonprofit organization operating in a unique private/public partnership with the City of Albuquerque.

THE INDIAN PUEBLO CULTURAL CENTER
2401 12th Street NW, Albuquerque, 843-7270
www.indianpueblo.org
Discounted admission for children and students. Children 7 and younger admitted free with an accompanying adult.

Traditional dances and festivals form the centerpiece of Pueblo Indian spiritual and cultural life, and this is a good place to see them. Performers come here from the 19 New Mexico Pueblos, from other New Mexico Indian tribes and elsewhere, representing a unique opportunity for visitors. Dances and public demonstrations by Native Amercian artists are scheduled often. Call the museum to learn if any dances are on the calendar during your visit.

The Cultural Center has museums, a restaurant, gallery and gift shop in addition to its outdoor dance plaza. The museum's unique focus is New Mexico's Pueblo Indian history and culture. Tracing the origins, spoken traditions, art and craftsmanship and the cultural development of these early New Mexicans, the center is a showcase for traditional art and culture and the creative adaptations that have ensured the Pueblo Indians' survival.

The Pueblo House Children's museum, open by appointment, offers an introduction to Pueblo history and culture for the younger set. Class tours are designed for school age children up to grade five. The tours provide students a variety of hands-on activities to enhance their overall learning experience. The museum holds a permanent exhibit that traces Pueblo Indian culture and history dating from the pre-Columbian era. The contemporary gallery showcases artisans from the 19 Pueblos featuring both traditional and contemporary craftsmanship.

The Pueblo Cultural Center opened in August, 1976, and attracts more than 200,000 visitors each year.

NATIONAL HISPANIC CULTURAL CENTER
1701 4th Street SW, Albuquerque, 246-2261
www.nhccnm.org
Children 16 and younger admitted free.

Creative Culture—The National Hispanic Cultural Center frequently hosts family-friendly events. *Photograph courtesy NHCC*

The purpose of the National Hispanic Cultural Center is to create a greater appreciation and understanding of Hispanic culture by preserving and showcasing historic and contemporary Hispanic arts, humanities, and achievements from the past 400 years.

The NHCC hosts Family Days/Community Days on weekends in the spring and fall, offering outdoor fun, live entertainment, hands-on arts and craft activities, storytellers, food booths, and often free books and school supplies. The most popular are *Día del Niño/ Cinco de Mayo*, the last weekend in April, and *Día de los Muertos* at the end of October/beginning of November.

Throughout the year NHCC offers concerts, hands-on art workshops in traditional and modern arts, summer movies for kids in English and Spanish and summer programs aimed at teens, including internships. The center hosts actors, musicians and storytellers from throughout Latin America and the U.S. NHCC includes the Roy E. Disney Center for Performing Arts, an art museum with a collection of Hispanic art and rotating exhibits from around the world, a gift shop and on-site restaurant.

THE LODESTAR ASTRONOMY CENTER
1801 Mountain Rd. NW, Albuquerque, 841-2800
LodeStar Information Hotline: 841-5955
www.lodestar.unm.edu/
Discounted tickets for children ages 3 to 12.
Children 2 and younger are free; children under 4 years of age
are not permitted in the Virtual Voyages simulation theater.

The LodeStar Astronomy Center, located in the New Mexico Museum of Natural History, has one of the newest planetariums in the world. The center presents state-of-the-art planetarium shows, a Virtual Voyages motion simulator ride and observatory events. The center's observatory houses a 16-inch telescope that, with the help of filtering lenses, provides safe daytime viewing of the sun for planetarium guests.

At the planetarium, visitors can watch The Search for Life, a full-dome planetarium feature developed by the American Museum of Natural History in collaboration with the National Aeronautic and Space Administration (NASA). The LodeStar planetarium, which houses the largest theater screen in New Mexico, is one of the only places in the world outside of New York's Hayden Planetarium where this 24-minute program, which talks about the possibility of life beyond Earth, can be seen. Elsewhere at Lodestar, visitors can learn about the constellations and planets visible in New Mexico's night sky and see images of space from the Hubble Telescope and NASA's space probes. The planetarium uses a projection system that makes it easier for audience members of all ages to see the stars and Milky Way.

Virtual Voyages, another attraction, is a high-energy theater experience, a motion-simulation ride that moves in six different directions. As you ride, you'll watch the prehistoric landscape of the Cretaceous world unfold through the eyes of seven different dinosaurs. You'll move with them as they interact in a realistic portrayal of their dangerous environment. (Riders must be at least four years old and three feet tall to ride Virtual Voyages.)

NEW MEXICO MUSEUM OF NATURAL HISTORY
AND SCIENCE
1801 Mountain Rd. N.W. Albuquerque 841-2800
www.nmnaturalhistory.org
Discounted tickets for ages 3-11; under 3 admitted free

More than Dinos—The New Mexico Museum of Natural History and Science also has a big-screen theater and a hands-on science center for kids and parents. *Photograph by Don Strel*

If you want to see dinosaurs, this is the spot!

From the formation of the universe to the present day, this large museum details the natural history of New Mexico and the Southwest, including lots of dinosaurs. You'll also find DynaTheater here with the largest movie screen in New Mexico. The LodeStar Astronomy Center, which shares the complex, has one of the newest planetariums in the world.

The museum has eight permanent exhibit halls that take visitors on a journey through time, providing snapshots of New Mexico from the formation of the universe to the present day. At the Naturalist Center, museum visitors can touch specimens and explore the natural world of New Mexico from snakes to fish. And stop at FossilWorks, a public display area where you can watch trained volunteers demonstrate the painstaking process of preparing fossils for display.

At the museum entrance, visitors are welcomed by two life-size New Mexico dinosaurs that were cast in bronze by Albuquerque sculptor Dave Thomas: Spike, the Pentaceratops and Alberta, the Albertosaurus. The Pentaceratops has been found only in New Mexico. Its name means five-horned lizard. Scientists first found the Albertosaurus in Alberta, Canada and since then have discovered its skeleton in New Mexico.

Dinosaurs lived in New Mexico for 159 million years, eras known as the Late Triassic, Jurassic and Cretaceous periods. Scientists working in New Mexico have found body fossils, or actual pieces of an animal, such as fossil bones and teeth. They have also discovered trace fossils such as footprints, skin impressions, egg shells, and coprolites—or fossilized dinosaur poop. New Mexico's history of dinosaurs covers nearly their entire existence, from their first appearance during the Late Triassic until their extinction at the end of the Cretaceous. Dinosaur fossils have been found across all of New Mexico except for the southeastern corner of the state. The New Mexico Museum of Natural History and Science holds the most dinosaurs on exhibit.

In addition to dinosaurs, the museum has a volcano, an exhibit on New Mexico's cave life and the skeleton of one of the world's largest birds, Diatryma. Camp-ins and a program for young docents encourage children to learn about New Mexico's natural history and have fun doing it.

RIO GRANDE BOTANIC GARDEN
2601 Central Avenue NW, Albuquerque, 764-6200
www.cabq.gov/biopark/garden
Discounted tickets for children; under 3 free.

Fantasy Garden—Plants, butterflies and special gardens for children entice visitors to Albuquerque's Botanic Garden.
Photo by Morys Hines courtesy of the Albuquerque Biological Park.

Located across the plaza from the Albuquerque Aquarium, the Rio Grande Botanic Garden features a special children's garden, indoor and outdoor gardens and plant displays on 20 developed acres.

Starting with a 14-foot high topiary dragon that guards the castle gates, the Children's Garden gives young visitors a larger-than-life perspective of plants, gardening and people. The garden entrance is a huge rabbit hole where mild-mannered 6-foot earthworms burrow through the walls. There are giant potted plants and huge soil particles that illustrate the difference between planting in sand and planting in clay. Don't miss the Nurse Tree complete with bird nest and kid-sized eggs. A seedling forest with enormous acorns and pinecones and a walk-through pumpkin 42 feet in diameter are among the other attractions.

The botanic garden includes a 10,000 square foot glass conservatory where you can see native and exotic plants from desert and Mediterranean climates. During the warm months, the butterfly conservatory showcases hundreds of free-flying North American butterflies and moths and thousands of the nectar plants they love.

The Rio Grande Heritage Farm, a 10-acre exhibit, invites visitors to take a trip back in time to farm life along the Rio Grande in the 1920s and 1930s. The exhibit features an adobe farmhouse, vineyard, apple orchards, field crops, small and large vegetable gardens and farm animals and equipment. In the adobe animal barn you'll meet Percheron draft horses, Alpine goats, Hampshire pigs, a Jersey cow, Churro sheep and Dominique chickens. Programs at this year-round working farm include interpretive presentations, hands-on demonstrations and farm activities.

Each winter, the garden hosts the River of Lights festival, which usually runs from the Saturday after Thanksgiving until the end of December. The display of lights includes wart hogs on the savanna, a three dimensional bee hive and lighted archways. A miniature garden railroad, complete with lighted model trains, cars, tracks, stations, trestles, bridges and a tiny village, operates every night. Hot food and beverages are available for purchase and live entertainment usually runs nightly until just before Christmas.

RIO GRANDE ZOO
903 10th Street SW, Albuquerque, 764-6200
www.cabq.gov/biopark/zoo/
Discounted admission for children;
free for children younger than three.

Dozens of Flamingos—In addition to flamingos, visitors to the Rio Grande Zoo can see many other birds and other animals of all sorts.
Photo by Robert Morin courtesy of the Albuquerque Biological Park

Founded in 1927, the 64-acre Rio Grande Zoo offers visitors encounters with more than 250 species of exotic and native animals. In the 1920s, Aldo Leopold, known as the "father of conservation," helped Albuquerque acquire and set aside land along the Rio Grande for Rio Grande State Park on which the zoo was constructed and still stands. At the zoo, you'll see gorillas, orangutans, elephants, and reptiles of all sorts. Don't miss the giraffes, camels, koalas,

Mexican wolves, mountain lions, monkeys, jaguars, zebras and rhinoceros. And then you have to devote some time watching the polar bears. Expect to spend at least three hours here.

The animals live in naturalistic habitats complete with trees, grasses, water features and rockwork. The zoo includes a rainforest greenhouse. Don't miss the 'cat walk', a trail that leads past all the major cat species including rare white tigers. You can see animals that usually come out at night, and, if you time it right, catch the seals enjoying their twice a day meal with underwater viewing.

The zoo's newest exhibits are Tropical America, a trip to the warm, damp climate where tropical animals and plants including toucans, spider monkeys, tamarins, orchids, tarantulas and colorful bromeliads live in a jungle-like fog. At the Gator Swamp exhibit in the ZooEd Kaleidoscope building you'll find very active baby American alligators. The swamp simulates the steamy, lush habitat of a southern bayou, complete with many varieties of orchid. The Naked Mole Rat Exhibit, also in the ZooEd building, offers view of the busy life of these unusual burrowing animals, native to parts of eastern Africa. Construction began in November, 2004, on a new Africa exhibit which will showcase African gazelles, red river hogs, zebras, chimpanzees and many more exotic animals. A narrow gauge railway will carry visitors in a loop through the exhibit.

In addition to the animals, the zoo offers World Animal Encounters from April through September. The show, free (with admission), is informative and entertaining featuring birds and endangered animals. During the summer for more than a decade the zoo has entertained visitors with the Zoo Music Concert Series. Zoo Music showcases regional, national and international talent under the band shell most Friday evenings in June, July and August. Known as a lively event where families can enjoy an evening of entertainment in a unique setting, the series has included Cajun, zydeco, bluegrass, Celtic, rock, jazz and more presented by regional, national and international talent.

SANDIA PEAK TRAMWAY
#10 Tramway Loop NE, Albuquerque, 856-7325
www.sandiapeak.com
Discounted tickets for children; under 5 ride for free

Ride the Tram—The view from the tram car will remind you of what you'd see from an airplane. *Photograph courtesy Sandia Peak Tramway*

The Sandia Peak Tramway, which advertises itself as the world's longest, takes visitors from the base of the rocky Sandia Mountains east of Albuquerque to their peak at 10,378 feet. From the top, known as Sandia Crest, you can see an 11,000 square mile panoramic view of New Mexico. The scene parallels what one might see from a very still airplane on a scenic flight. The Tram has taken more than 6 million passengers to the top of Sandia Peak and back again since it opened in 1966. It is one of the biggest tourist attractions in Central New Mexico.

Passengers lift off from the desert floor in one of two 50-person glass walled tram cars. The tram soars above canyons and lush forest to the mountain top in a 2.7 mile trip that takes about 15 minutes. Passengers ascend 4,000 feet, gliding along the western face of the rugged Sandia Mountains, past granite eroded into spires, cliffs and pinnacles. Tram riders may see an eagle, a mule deer or perhaps a black bear as they look out. From the top, you can look west, over the city of Albuquerque and across the Rio Grande and a volcano field to see Mount Taylor rise more than 70 miles away. To the north you'll spot Cabezon, a stump of an eroded volcano, and other volcanic necks and plugs. To the east lies the heavily wooded backside of the Sandias and, on the far horizon, the Sangre de Cristo Mountains and Santa Fe.

From the tram station at the top of Sandia Peak, passengers may hike along the forest trails observing the rock formations, natural vegetation and wildlife. The tram serves Sandia Peak Ski Area, a prime spot for intermediate and beginning skiers from mid December through mid March. During the summer, the chairlift offers a lovely ride through the towering trees. Sandia Peak has more than 26 miles of trails for mountain bikers with easy access via the chairlift for riders and their vehicles. There is a restaurant at the top of the tramway.

DAY TRIPS: LOS ALAMOS

Bandelier and More—Los Alamos, a 45 minute drive from Santa Fe, includes many interesting attractions and is near Bandelier National Monument.
Photograph by Lynne Dominy, National Park Service

LOS ALAMOS HISTORICAL MUSEUM
1921 Juniper Street, Los Alamos, 662-6272
www.vla.com/Historicalsociety
Free

BRADBURY SCIENCE MUSEUM
15th and Central Avenue, Los Alamos, 667-4444
www.lanl.gov/worldview/museum
Free

LOS ALAMOS DEMONSTRATION GARDEN
Central at Oppenheimer, 662-2656
Free

VALLES CALDERA NATIONAL PRESERVE
20 miles west of Los Alamos on NM 4, 661-3333
www.vallescaldera.gov
Admission fees vary

(Please see separate entry on Bandelier National Monument)

This trip, especially recommended for children of mid-school age or older, offers an introduction to New Mexico's contribution to our atomic age and a look at the area's fascinating geology. Los Alamos is a 45-minute drive north and west of Santa Fe.

Los Alamos sits in a dramatically beautiful location on the colorful mesas that extend from the wooded slopes of the Jemez Mountains to the west. The town of about 17,000 people overlooks the Rio Grande Valley and, to the east beyond, the peaks of the Sangre de Cristo range, which form the southern end of the Rocky Mountains.

The logical place to start is the Historical Museum, a small, charmingly old-fashioned sort of museum which offers an introduction to the geology and anthropology of the area as well as information on Los Alamos before the Manhattan Project which led to the development of the atomic bomb. The museum exhibits artifacts of early Pajarito Plateau dwellers as well as displays from the Los Alamos National Laboratory's wartime era. You'll learn how and why the Jemez Volcano erupted 1.4 million years ago and can walk through an exhibit about wartime Los Alamos, "Life in the Secret City." The museum also hosts changing exhibits.

Afterwards, it's just a short walk to the Bradbury Science Museum.

This large, bright space displays exhibits about the history of Los Alamos National Laboratory and its research. Many of the exhibits are interactive and feature videos, computers, and science demonstrations. The museum's goal is to serve as a bridge between the laboratory and the community, helping to improve science education and science literacy. The museum also interprets the laboratory's history and current research. More than 40 high-tech interactive exhibits within five galleries explain the laboratory's defense, technology, and basic research projects, as well as the history of the Manhattan Project which led to the development of the first atomic bomb. A 20-minute film on the history of the race to build the atomic bomb at Los Alamos runs throughout the day. During weekdays, science educators give live, hands-on science demonstrations for visitors and school groups.

The museum's Research and Technology galleries include The Environment Exhibit which shows how the laboratory is solving problems relating to energy, waste disposal, air pollution, and global warming. Included are plants that remove hazardous waste from the soil, bacteria that digest TNT, new methods to improve automobile efficiency and new sources of energy. The Life Sciences Exhibit includes information about genetics illustrated with interactive computer programs. An exhibit on lasers explains how they work and ways scientists are using lasers in research from medical technology to defense.

After the museum, you may want to take a look at the Los Alamos Demonstration Garden, which offers a chance to learn about gardening in a high altitude, semiarid environment. You can stroll among colorful flowers, trees and shrubs and learn about fire-defensible landscaping, water harvesting, invasive weeds and plants that stimulate the senses. The Los Alamos Master Gardeners Club maintains the garden, which covers 1.5 acres, or nearly two city blocks, on the north side of town.

The garden includes a model fire-defensible landscape with a small cabin made of noncombustible materials to show how to protect homes located near forests. The cabin's water-harvesting features show visitors how to maximize use of rainwater. Other sections includes fruit trees that grow well in high altitudes and areas that allow visitors to touch, smell and even taste a variety of low-water-use plants. A visual flower bed highlights brightly-colored plants such as yellow goldenrod and evening primrose, red cardinals, pink twirling butterflies and purple aster. The garden is designed for easy wheelchair and stroller access, including wide paths and raised beds. Solar-powered lights have been added for nighttime visits, along with wooden stands with information about the plants in each section. A central patio has wooden benches and an overhead structure for shade.

If your schedule allows, don't miss The Valles Caldera National Preserve, 20 miles west of Los Alamos. Uses for this vast expanse of publicly owned land—approximately 89,000 acres—are still in the planning stage, but you may hike the Valle Grande Trail and Coyote Call Trail without advance reservation or fee. If snowfall allows, the preserve is also open for cross-country skiing and snowshoeing, payment at the door.

BANDELIER NATIONAL MONUMENT
45 miles NW of Santa Fe on State Highway 4, 672-3861
www.nps.gov/band
Admission by carload fee

Ladders and Caves—Bandelier National Monument welcomes families with an easy trail that leads to the ruins. *Photograph by Lynne Dominy, National Park Service*

This popular park, known for mesas, sheer-walled canyons and ancestral Pueblo dwellings is filled with ancient, cave-style cliff residences and Indian ruins. There's a lot for families to explore here. In the process, you'll get an idea of what life was like more than a thousand years ago. Bandelier, named for 19th-century anthropologist Adolph Bandelier, includes more than 23,000 acres of designated wilderness. The relatives of some of today's Pueblo Indians lived here from the 12th century to the mid-1500s.

The park was established in 1916 and has been drawing visitors ever since. You may find a crowd at the peak of the summer visitor season, but you can come here year round. Your family can tour the monument on a self-guided path, or join up with a ranger. (Call for information about guided tours and moonlight visits.)

Most visitors start with the one-mile interpretative Main Loop Trail, which leads from the visitor center through excavated archeological sites, places where the Indians slept, cooked and conducted their spiritual ceremonies. You'll have an opportunity to climb ladders, enter caves where the Indians once lived, walk on narrow trails through the rock and see ancient rock carvings. The main loop trail provides a good sampling of the structures used by these ancient people, as well as rock drawings, all in a beautiful natural setting. The loop is stroller and wheelchair accessible.

For the more adventurous, the national monument offers 65 miles of trails, including hikes to other archaeological sites in the canyon. The trails vary from short and easy to long and strenuous. Ask at the visitor center before heading out. The park also offers interpretive talks and evening programs. On summer weekends you might find a crafts demonstration with a guest Indian or Hispanic artist on hand to make turkey feather blankets, paint gourds, or create pottery or jewelry, wood carvings or other traditional crafts. Please contact the monument office for a schedule and more information.

Bandelier is open year round. Be sure to wear sturdy shoes and bring food and water if you intend to do more extensive exploring here.

DAY TRIPS: ELSEWHERE

KASHA-KATUWE TENT ROCKS and COCHITI LAKE

TENT ROCKS: 40 miles southwest of Santa Fe
(see directions below), 438-7400 (BLM)
www.nm.blm.gov/aufo/tent_rocks/tent_rocks.html
Visitation charge per vehicle.

This day trip introduces you to a great place to hike and a lake where you can swim or fish. The unusual rock formations cover almost 12,000 acres, providing a surreal background for an easy day hike. The lake, built by the Corps of Engineers, is favored by windsurfers.

At Tent Rocks, you'll see light-colored rock formations which are the products of volcanic eruptions that occurred between 6 and 7 million years ago. The cone-shapes show the effects of wind and water on the soft stone. The hard, erosion-resistant caprocks protect the tent shapes below. On the hike, you'll pass by ancient rocks shaped by centuries of wind and rain. The Kasha-Katuwe park, or "white cliffs" in Keresan—the traditional language for the nearby Pueblo de Cochiti—features tent-shaped rocks created by the powerful forces of volcanic activity and eons of erosion. The area is rich in pumice, ash, and tuff deposits.

Because the trail can be steep and narrow, strollers and baby carriers don't work well here, but children old enough to enjoy walking will love the twists and turns through narrow rock canyons. Wear sturdy shoes, and bring food and lots of drinking water, especially in the summer. No climbing is permitted on the rock formations.

Kasha-Katuwe Tent Rocks is 40 miles southwest of Santa Fe, with the most direct access from Interstate 25. Take the Cochiti

Reservoir exit from I-25 to State Road 22 and follow the signs to Cochiti Pueblo. Turn right at the pueblo water tower (painted like a drum) onto Tribal Route 92 (connects to Forest Service Road 266). Travel 5 miles on a dirt road to the parking area, which is marked with a sign. This is the only parking area for Kasha-Katuwe Tent Rocks.

COCHITI LAKE
82 Dam Crest Rd., Pena Blanca, N.M. 465-0307
(40 miles south of Santa Fe via I-25 and NM 22)

Nearby Cochiti Lake is a 1200 square mile no-wake lake impounded behind one of the largest earth dams in the world. Facilities include a paved boat ramp and campground with showers. The top water activities here are sailing, wind surfing, swimming and fishing. You'll find electrical hookups, picnic sites, group shelters, restrooms/showers and drinking water. The Pueblo de Cochiti operates and maintains a small marina here. A visitor center sits on the west side of the lake.

PECOS NATIONAL HISTORIC PARK
Two miles south of the village of Pecos, N.M. on N.M. highway 63.
757-6414 www.nps.gov/peco
Children 16 and younger are admitted free.

Pecos National Monument—A visit to this historic site, a short drive from Santa Fe, offers a look at Pueblo Indian and early Spanish life in New Mexico.
Artwork courtesy of Curt Hawley.

This national park preserves 12,000 years of history including the ancient pueblo of Pecos, two Spanish Colonial missions, Santa Fe Trail sites, a 20th century ranch and the site of the Civil War Battle of Glorieta Pass. The ruins trail, picnic area, and visitor center are open to visitors. Other park sites, such as the Forked Lightning Ranch, once owned by actress Greer Garson, the Santa Fe Trail, and the Civil War Battlefield of Glorieta are available only through ranger-guided tours. (To schedule a tour, please contact the visitor center.)

The visitor center contains exhibits about early New Mexico and a 10-minute introductory film. The self-guided trail through the Pecos pueblo and mission ruins is a little over a mile walk and takes you to kivas, or Indian ceremonial structures, and ruins of a Spanish church. Pecos was a pivotal spot in New Mexico's history, a vital trading center for the Plains Indian and an important stop on the Santa Fe Trail. A major battle of the Civil War was fought near here. Summer programs include weekend cultural demonstrations. You can picnic near mission ruins; the average stay is one to two hours.

The park is easy to find, 25 miles east of Santa Fe off Interstate 25, which follows some of the route of the Old Santa Fe Trail.

The community of Pecos, just a few miles from the park, is a gateway to the Pecos Wilderness in the Sangre de Cristo range of the southern Rockies. The wilderness beyond the town includes 223,333 acres of peaks, forests, lakes, streams and mountain meadows. You'll find fly fishing in mountain streams and lakes and great spots for hiking, picnics and exploration. The Jack's Creek/Iron Gate and Aspen Basin trailheads are especially popular. You can rent horses or arrange for a hunting or fishing guide in Pecos or the little town of Tererro a few miles north of Pecos.

PUEBLO INDIAN VILLAGES NEAR SANTA FE

Several Indian pueblos, or villages, are within easy driving distance of Santa Fe.

Visitors are welcome on most days of the year at most pueblos. The best time to visit is during a dance or other special events open to the public. Dances are held on the feast day of the Catholic saint who is the pueblo's patron. Many pueblos also hold dances on Christmas Eve and Christmas Day, New Year's Day, Jan. 6 (the Christian feast of the Three Kings) and Easter.

A good source for information on Pueblo dances is the Indian Pueblo Cultural Center in Albuquerque (843-7270, www.indianpueblo.com), which can help you learn more about the culture and history of the Pueblo Indians. (Look for it in our Day Trips section.) Each of the 19 pueblos is represented in displays of weaving, pottery, jewelry, clothing and photographghraphy. You'll also find information and a beautiful collection of Pueblo arts and crafts at the Museum of Indian Arts and Culture. (See our Places to Visit section.) Most of New Mexico's pueblos operate casinos. The gambling areas are closed to children, but some allow children to attend concerts or eat in the restaurants.

The Pueblo of Taos is one of New Mexico's most authentic examples of pueblo architecture and tradition. The pueblo's much photographed multistory apartment houses and famous church are about 75 miles from Santa Fe. Taos Pueblo traditionally closes to the public for much of March and April.

Pueblo Etiquette

All the state's pueblos are small villages, traditional homes to the Indian families; not reconstructed tourist destinations. Please observe all posted requests and regulations. Be aware that public restrooms may not be available. Do not take your pets.

If you are fortunate enough to attend a Pueblo Feast Day dance or other dance open to the public, remember that the tradition is a deeply spiritual observance, not a festival put on for tourists. Be as respectful as you would be visiting a cathedral. Native children often participate in dances as part of their cultural training; visiting children need to watch with respectful attention.

If photography is allowed, please maintain a respectful distance from dancers and drummers. Dances are prayers in motion and require concentration on the part of the dancers, so quiet is appreciated. Applause is considered inappropriate as is dancing along with the dancers. Laptops and cell phones should be left in the car or at home.

Each pueblo has different rules about sketching, photography and video taping; many do not allow it. Be sure to ask what is allowed and follow the rules. Do not let children wander unattended, climb on walls or look into windows. Do not allow them to walk into graveyards, pick up rocks or remove anything.

Here are a few other basic principals of Pueblo etiquette:

- Do not ask questions about the meaning of the dancing, costumes or music and refrain from talking to the dancers or singers until the dancing is done for the day. Do not cross the plaza (dance area) or walk between the dancers, singers or drummers.
- Enter a house only by invitation.
- It is an honor to be invited to eat at a Pueblo home after a dance. If you receive an invitation, do not refuse even if you have already eaten or are not hungry! After you've finished, please make room for the next guest; do not linger at the table.
- At some pueblos you'll find galleries and artists' studios. These will have signs and may state visiting hours.
- Drive carefully and watch for children and animals.

- Never enter kivas, the underground ceremonial chambers. These are sacred.
- Leave all pottery shards, rocks or any other natural formations where you find them.
- If you are on a guided tour, please stay with your group.

Cultural Tradition—Pueblo children participate in dances at the Eight Northern Pueblos Arts and Crafts show and at tribal feast days. *Photograph by Don Strel*

A simplified Pueblo directory:

Here is contact information for some of the pueblos near Santa Fe. We've selected these because they have museums, buffalo herds, fishing lakes or other attractions of special interest to young visitors. Please check with the pueblos for more information.

Jemez
7413 Hwy 4 Jemez Pueblo, NM 87024
834-7235 (Visitor Center)
834-7359 (Governor)
About 75 miles southwest of Santa Fe

Nambe
Route 1 Box 117-BB
Santa Fe NM 87501
455-2036
About 23 miles north of Santa Fe

Picuris
PO Box 127
Peñasco, NM 87553
587-2519
About 60 miles northeast of Santa Fe

Pojoaque
Route 11 Box 21-GS
Santa Fe, NM 87501
455-3460 (Tourist Center)
455-3901 (Governor)
15 miles north of Santa Fe

Sandia
PO Box 6008
Bernalillo, NM 87004
867-3317
www.sandiapueblo.nsn.us
50 miles southwest of Santa Fe

San Ildefonso
Route 5 Box 315-A
Santa Fe, NM 87506
455-3549 (Visitor Center)
455-2273 (Governor)
23 miles northwest of Santa Fe

San Juan
PO Box 1099
San Juan Pueblo, NM 87566
852-4400 (Governor)
30 miles north of Santa Fe

Santa Clara
PO Box 580
Española, NM 87532
753-7326 (Tourism Office)
753-7330 (Governor)
22 miles northwest of Santa Fe

Taos
PO Box 1846
Taos, NM 87571
758-1028 (Tourism Office)
73 miles northeast of Santa Fe

SANTA FE SOUTHERN RAILWAY
410 S. Guadalupe Street, 989-8600,
(800) 989-8600, or (888) 989-8600
www.sfsr.com
Discounted tickets for children age 2 and younger ride free.

For a leisurely look at the landscape of the Santa Fe plateau and the vast Galisteo Basin, try a train ride. The Santa Fe Southern Railway departs from the Santa Fe Depot, rebuilt in 1909 after the original was destroyed in a fire. The antique train cars, including luxury coaches and an open-air platform, will take you out to the countryside where you'll see panoramic views of Northern New Mexico's high desert ringed by the blue Jémez, Sandia and Sangre de Cristo mountains. The views extend for up to 120 miles. The train, which once served as a spur of the Atchison, Topeka & Santa Fe Railway, covers the 36-mi round-trip scenic jaunt to Lamy, a sleepy village with the region's only Amtrak service, in four and a half hours including a stopover for a picnic. You can bring your own lunch or dinner or buy one from the caterer who meets the train, and enjoy it beneath the cottonwoods at the quaint rail station. Aside from day trips, the railway offers special events such as a summer "Sunset Run," on which a barbecue, a campfire, and live entertainment await you at the Lamy depot. In the winter you'll find holiday excursions including Santa Claus trains.

WILDLIFE WEST NATURE PARK
Edgewood, 281-7655 or toll-free 877-981-9453
www.frontpage.swcp.com/~wildlife
Discounts for children; younger than 5 admitted free.

Wildlife West, an educational project of the New Mexico Wildlife Association, is a 122-acre wildlife refuge and zoo east of the Sandia Mountains between Santa Fe and Albuquerque. All the animals and birds cared for here are non-releasable, which means they could not survive without the help of people. The park is staffed by volunteers and members of the New Mexico Youth Conservation Corps. Attractions include the Wild Bird Nature Trail, native plants, and elk, deer, bobcat, mountain lion, foxes, raccoons, turtle, ducks and raptors.

The park offers a summer camp for junior zoo keepers and bird handling classes. With special reservations, you can have an overnight adventure with wolves and cougars. Weekends bring family celebrations including Bluegrass Sundays and the Wildlife West chuckwagon dinner shows on Saturday nights, with food and music.

To reach the park from Santa Fe, go south on NM 14 to Tijeras, then east on I-40 to exit 187 (Edgewood). At the end of the exit ramp, turn north on the north frontage road. Continue three-fourths of a mile until you see the entrance to the park on the right.

Wildlife West is open all year.

SPECIAL EVENTS FOR KIDS AND FAMILIES

n introduction.

In this chapter you'll learn about some things to do in Santa Fe and Albuquerque, most of which happen only once a year. The event listings include big community-wide celebrations like the Santa Fe Fiesta, Indian Market and Spanish Market. Although both the markets are primarily designed to sell the artists' work, families can watch artists as they demonstrate their skill and admire work done by children. Other events, such as the Sun Mountain Gathering, are more "hands-on" and designed to attract families with layers of activities suitable for all ages and interests.

One thing certain about Santa Fe is that it's always changing. If you're planning a visit, please check with the Santa Fe visitors' website, www.santafe.org, for an updated calendar. And don't forget to use the local newspapers and the area's special publications for children, Tumbleweeds and New Mexico Kids, as further resources. The city is rich with spontaneous happenings!

The events which follow are in rough chronological order. We didn't give dates because things change, but indicated the approximate time frame such as "third weekend in July." And, if you notice something we've left out, please let us know so we can include it in the next edition.

(All area codes are 505 unless indicated otherwise. If admission is free, or discounts are offered for children, we noted it.)

Getting Ready—These young men are carving for the Traditional Spanish Market, one of many Santa Fe events which welcome families.
Photograph by Patricia Price, Museum of Spanish Colonial Art

SANTA FE

MAY

BACKSTAGE PASS
Santa Fe Opera, 7 miles north of the downtown Santa Fe Plaza on U.S. Highway 84/285
986-5955
www.santafeopera.org/commprograms/backpass
Free

Opera Open House—The Santa Fe Opera welcomes children and parents each May at its annual open house. The event includes performances by children and tours of the Santa Fe Opera costume shop. *Photo by Bob Godwin, courtesy The Santa Fe Opera*

Held on a Saturday in May, Backstage Pass is the world-famous Santa Fe Opera's annual community open house. The "Pass" means that areas normally off limits to the public are open with guided tours. Everyone, young and old, can see the myriad of fascinating elements that go into each opera production. You get to peek into the way opera magic is made. Visitors can take a look at a gallery of Santa Fe Opera costumes and visit the scene shop where the sets are made and the intriguing prop shop. Learn about the remarkable history and vision that has made The Santa Fe Opera one of the nation's top opera companies.

    Entertainment adds to the fun, with student-produced operas performed by children and teens from Santa Fe and elsewhere. There's usually a concert performance by Opera Mosaic, a group of professional players who present opera in the schools. You can picnic on the opera grounds, a grassy oasis in the arid foothills of Santa Fe. Drinks and picnic food such as hot dogs and Frito pies are for sale. Be sure to bring a hat and sunscreen. Admission is free thanks to the Guilds of The Santa Fe Opera Inc. which host the annual event.

SPRING, SUMMER AND FALL

PLAZA ARTS AND CRAFTS SHOWS
Downtown on the Plaza and surrounding streets, 983-7317
www.santafe.org
Free

In addition to Santa Fe's major summer art shows, Spanish Market in July and Indian Market in August, you'll find more art on the Plaza. Several other times including mid-June, early August and Labor Day weekend, the Plaza sprouts colorful booths filled with even more colorful arts and crafts. The free shows usually feature a wide range of first-rate painting, jewelry, photography, sculpture, weaving and ceramics both useful and decorative. You may find handmade clothing, original toys, stained glass and other arts and crafts from all disciplines. The shows offer adults and children a chance to see a variety of beautiful creations in many price ranges in a relaxed, outdoor setting. You can chat with the artisans if you wish. Food and live music sometimes add to the weekend festivities.

To be featured in any Plaza show, artists have to submit their work to a jury and may sit on the waiting list before they get one of the coveted spaces. (Please see information on Spanish Market and Indian Market elsewhere in this section.)

FESTIVALS AND THEME WEEKENDS
El Rancho de las Golondrinas
334 Los Pinos Road, La Cienega, 471-2261
www.golondrinas.org
Children under 5 usually free. Discounts for children and teens.

Festivals Galore—El Rancho de las Golondrinas hosts a variety of festivals and special events. *Photograph courtesy El Rancho de las Golondrinas*

A living history museum, El Rancho de las Golondrinas buzzes with family-friendly weekend programs in the spring, summer and fall. During the festivals you may have a chance to watch:

- A blacksmith and wheelwright at work
- Carding, spinning, washing and dyeing wool
- Weaving typical rugs, cloth and blankets
- Animal events and animal care demonstrations
- Soap, candle and rope making

- Leather and woodworking
- Grinding corn and wheat by hand and with water mills
- Making and baking bread and cookies in the *hornos*, or outdoor ovens
- Other activities with costumed volunteers taking the roles of old-time rancher families.

The museum sits on 200 acres filled with 18th century buildings, a shady mill pond and plenty of animals. The complex includes old houses, blacksmith shops, water-powered mills, a chapel and a winery. A visit requires some walking, so wear sturdy shoes and bring water and sunscreen. In addition to the activities mentioned here, the museum may have other exciting things on its calendar. Food is available at most of these events.

In June, the Spring Festival and Animal Fair gives families an up-close look at shearing *churro* sheep on a Spanish colonial ranch and many other skills of daily life re-enacted by friendly, well-informed volunteers in village costumes. Music, dance, art, and other entertainment are part of the fun.

In August, the museum hosts its Summer Festival & Frontier Days. A performance by the exotic Peruvian Paso horses and a chance to visit with volunteers taking the roles of mountain men, soldiers, traders and gunfighters mark the event. The museum comes to life with activities for the whole family.

Also in August, look for Uniquely New Mexico: Food, Art & Adobe, a festival devoted to the sights, aromas and tastes of traditional colonial cuisine. Children can learn how to make and build with *adobes*, or traditional mud bricks. Lessons in creating a *retable*, a hand-painted expression of spiritual art, are part of the weekend celebration.

In September, don't miss the *Fiesta de los Niños*, A Celebration for Children. You'll find historic games and activities for youngsters and adults.

Glorious Golondrinas—El Rancho de las Golondrinas brings a historic ranch to life with the help of volunteers of all ages. *Photo courtesy El Rancho de las Golondrinas*

In early October the ranch presents the Harvest Festival, a major event which brings the museum to life with reenactments of everyday activities common in the colonial era as preparation for winter. Children may get a chance to crush grapes for wine, sample home-baked bread and taste fresh sorghum molasses. Volunteers clothed in the styles of the times spin yarn, shoe horses, tend the animals, chat with visitors and do other things that were part of life in early New Mexico. You'll also find old-time music, dancing, costumed riders on horseback, food and arts and crafts for sale.

In addition to these activities, the museum often presents other special events. Please check their website for updated calendars.

JUNE

RODEO DE SANTA FE
3237 Rodeo Road, 471-4300
www.rodeodesantafe.org
Free parade
Discounts for children in some seating areas

Junior Wranglers—Rodeo de Santa Fe offers events especially for children including mutton "busting." *Photograph by Martin Moya*

Held in late June, the Rodeo de Santa Fe is a long-established attraction which draws cowboys from the region and beyond. Performances extend over several days and include individual and team roping, steer wrestling, barrel racing, saddle and bareback bronc riding and, the audience favorite, bull riding. Clowns and visiting specialty acts such as dancing horses and trained dogs add to the fun. Kids can try their hand at a calf scramble and mutton busting, where children try to ride gentle but uncooperative sheep. The rodeo usually offers the children's competitions both before and during each evening rodeo performance and a calf scramble for older wranglers at the Saturday matinee. Reservations for kids who want to participate are taken, first-come, first-served and a fee is charged for the chance to catch a calf or ride a sheep.

    The rodeo opens with a parade around the Plaza featuring bands, antique cars, floats and, of course, horses galore.

ANNUAL WEST MUTTSTER DOG SHOW
Alto Park, 1043 Alto Street, 983-4309
www.sfhumanesociety.org/index.html
Free

Dogs don't need a pedigree for this show, but they might need a costume!

The Santa Fe Animal Shelter and Humane Society sponsors this highly informal day of fun, usually on a Sunday in mid-June, as a reunion for dogs that have gone to good homes thanks to the shelter's work. The dog show is also a celebration of all the good dogs adopted from humane societies or rescue groups. (Sorry, no cats allowed.)

Contests in the past have included most mixed, dog and owner look-alikes, old dog, new trick/new dog, old trick, most extraordinary tail, most spots and "stands out in a crowd." Dog obedience demonstrations, music, food and face painting add to the mix. This outdoor event, and the weather can be hot. Dogs also are welcome as observers, no matter where they came from.

JULY

PANCAKE BREAKFAST
The Plaza
United Way of Santa Fe, 982-2002
www.uwsfc.org/news_and_events/pancakes_on_the_plaza.html
Discounted tickets for children

Fun on the 4th—United Way's Pancakes on the Plaza is a community tradition with music and dance on the menu. *Photograph courtesy United Way of Santa Fe County*

Come down to the Santa Fe Plaza on the Fourth of July. Food is the centerpiece of this day of community celebration, a fund-raiser for United Way of Santa Fe County. Hundreds of volunteers cook pancakes and ham and serve them up with coffee, orange juice and milk. A varied program of entertainment, from mariachis to the Santa Fe Concert Band, performs for free on the bandstand. Before or after breakfast, be sure to take a look at the well-kept antique cars, presented by Santa Fe Vintage Car Club, that line the streets. Some years arts and crafts booths are also part of the fun.

Tickets for the pancake breakfast are available in advance from the sponsor, United Way of Santa Fe, or on the Plaza the day of the event.

NAMBE FALLS CEREMONIAL
Nambe Pueblo, 20 miles north of Santa Fe
455-2036

Another Fourth of July treat is the Nambe Falls Ceremonial, held at Nambe Pueblo, about 20 miles north of Santa Fe. The celebration, which takes place at the waterfall, features various Native American dances and an arts and crafts show. While you're there, you might spot the pueblo's buffalo herd. Please call the pueblo ahead of time for information on dance times and admission fees.

SANTA FE INTERNATIONAL FOLK ART MARKET
Milner Plaza, Museum Hill (Camino Lejo), 476-1203
www.folkartmarket.org

Intercultural Experience—The Santa Fe International Folk Art Market includes entertainment. *Photograph courtesy Museum of New Mexico*

Children love the energy of this event which features master folk artists from around the globe gathered on scenic Milner Plaza outside the Museum of International Folk Art. The festival, a multicultural, multi-media celebration, gives visitors the rare opportunity to see and purchase beautiful handmade craftwork from around the world. Music, demonstrations of various folk art techniques and hands-on children's activities are part of the fun. The non-profit market, inaugurated in 2004, is presented by the Museum of International Folk Art and the Museum of New Mexico Foundation. Please check with the museum for the exact dates.

The market is a treasure house of traditional arts and crafts. Previous shows have included hand-embroidered textiles from Bangladesh, apparel from Uzbekistan, pillows from Sweden, Arabian handicrafts, hand-carved gourds from Peru and tribal beadwork from Africa. Among the finds, you'll spot dolls, toys and gifts for children.

The event has been sponsored by The Kellogg Foundation, McCune Charitable Foundation, the New Mexico Department of Tourism, St. John's College and UNESCO.

EIGHT NORTHERN INDIAN PUEBLOS
ARTS AND CRAFTS SHOW
San Juan Pueblo Showgrounds, Espanola, N.M.
PO Box 969, San Juan Pueblo, N. M., 87566, 747-1593
Discounted admission for children

Pueblo Show—The eight Northern Pueblos Arts and Crafts Show often highlights dancing by youth groups. *Photograph by Don Strel*

Featuring more than 300 Native American artists and craftspeople, this outdoor show and sale includes Native American dances, music and food. Watch for it the third weekend in July. Operated by the Pueblos themselves, it is the premier event of its kind in the world. The display of unique, hand-crafted traditional and contemporary Native American art draws visitors from throughout the United States and elsewhere. In addition to art by adult artists, the show features the work of children in a special booth.

In addition to visual attractions, the show includes a showcase of traditional Indian dances presented every half hour to the compelling rhythms of Native American music. Dances such as the Buffalo Dance, Deer Dance, Rainbow Dance and Corn Dance, accompanied by singers and drummers are performed by dancers from different pueblos and tribes. Children's dance groups are often part of the entertainment.

In conjunction with the show, the Eight Northern Indian Pueblos Council also present the annual PoPay foot race, held in honor of the first and only Indian uprising which succeeded in driving European conquerors out of Indian territory for more than 10 years. The race has a special children's category.

Organized by the Eight Northern Indian Pueblo Council, representing Tesuque, San Juan, San Ildefonso, Santa Clara, Nambe, Pojoaque, Taos and Picuris Pueblos, the festival began in 1972 with 100 artists. Today, the Eight Northern Indian Pueblos Arts and Crafts Show is one of the most popular events in New Mexico, attracting top artisans and thousands of visitors each summer. This is an outdoor event on natural terrain and visitors should be prepared with hats, proper shoes, sunscreen and light clothing.

MUSIC ON THE PLAZA
Santa Fe Plaza sponsored by the Santa Fe Arts Commission,
955-6706
www.santafenm.gov
Free

Visitors and residents are invited to relax on the Santa Fe plaza and listen to local bands and traveling musicians. Music on the Plaza, a long-time summer tradition, presents free concerts several afternoons and evenings a week, usually in July and August. Entertainment ranges from rock and jazz to blues and zydeco. Some listeners bring a picnic dinner. The arts commission can provide an up-to-date schedule.

TRADITIONAL SPANISH MARKET AND CONTEMPORARY HISPANIC MARKET
On the Plaza and on adjacent streets, 982-2226, 983-4038
www.spanishmarket.org
Free

Spanish Tradition—The Traditional Spanish Market include budding artists.
Photograph by Jack Parsons courtesy Museum of Spanish Colonial Art

Traditionally held the last weekend in July, the annual Traditional Spanish Market celebrates and honors the artistic heritage of the Hispanic culture of Northern New Mexico. Concurrently with the traditional market is the contemporary Hispanic Market, open to artists working in non-traditional forms. The traditional work is displayed on the Plaza; the contemporary art in booths on adjoining Lincoln Avenue. (Don't worry—you'll easily know the difference.) Many of the artists featured here don't show in galleries.

The oldest and largest exhibition and sale of Spanish colonial art forms in the United States, Spanish Market features more than 300 traditional Hispanic artists, and includes special categories for young people. Continuous live music, art demonstrations and regional foods are part of this opportunity to enjoy a taste of New Mexico's vibrant Spanish culture, both past and present.

The traditional art forms featured each year at Spanish Market include both secular and religious art. The market usually presents a large variety of *santos*, or depictions of religious figures in the forms of *bultos* (carvings in the round), *retablos* (paintings on wooden panels), and gesso and wood relief-carved panels. You'll see booths with paintings on deer or elk hide; straw appliqué work decorating crosses, chests and boxes and tinwork, along with textiles, furniture, *colcha*-style embroidery, iron work, baskets, jewelry and pottery.

In addition to art, the market showcases musical performers in Northern New Mexico. Artist demonstrations are part of the weekend's events. A calendar of entertainment is available at the show, on the website or from the newspapers.

Besides the traditional summer market, the Spanish Colonial Arts Society which sponsors the event also hosts an indoor winter market each December.

MOUNTAIN MAN TRADE FAIR RENDEZVOUS
Palace of the Governors Courtyard, 105 W Palace Ave. 476-5100
http://www.palaceofthegovernors.org
Free

In early or mid-August, costumed mountain men ride into town on horseback, heading for the Museum of New Mexico's annual Mountain Man Rendezvous. The event is a recreation of a large gathering of trappers and traders held in towns like Santa Fe in the early 19th century. Participants, dressed in colorful costumes, sell antique and reproduction tools, arts and crafts and objects the frontier settlers would have depended on for survival. The fair includes competitions from the old days such as knife and tomahawk throwing, muzzleloader rifle shooting, cannon firing, storytelling, music and foot races.

AUGUST

ICE CREAM SUNDAY
Santa Fe Children's Museum, 1050 Old Pecos Trail, 989-8359
www.santafechildrensmuseum.org

This annual party and fund-raiser, traditionally held the first Sunday in August, begins at noon and continues through late afternoon or until the ice cream runs out. Santa Fe celebrities, including the mayor, the superintendent of schools and the chief of police, have helped with the scooping. Visitors can make their own sundaes or banana splits. Besides the ice cream, the museum provides free entertainment. All the money goes for new exhibits at the museum, the only one in Santa Fe dedicated to children.

SANTA FE BLUEGRASS AND OLD TIME MUSIC FESTIVAL
Santa Fe Rodeo Grounds, 3237 Rodeo Road, 438-6230, 298-3080
(Albuquerque)
www.southwestpickers.org
Children under 14 free

For more than 20 years, the Southwest Traditional and Bluegrass Music Association Festival has brought banjo and fiddle music to Santa Fe for a long weekend in late August or early September.

The festival features concerts, workshops and special events and a lot of informal fun, too. Among the highlights are original songs and appearances by the prior year's winners in the Bluegrass Band and Old Timey Band contests. The festival includes a special two-hour children's workshop which invites kids to make music with other kids under guidance and with instrumental backup from adults. As part of the festival, the grounds are open to campers, a tradition which leads to a lot of informal after-hours jamming. The festival includes opening concerts Friday night, music all day Saturday and a Sunday function. Local, regional and national traditional and bluegrass bands join in the celebration. You'll also find vendors with CDs galore and festival foods.

SANTA FE COUNTY FAIR
Santa Fe County Fair Grounds, 3229 Rodeo Road, 471-4711
Free

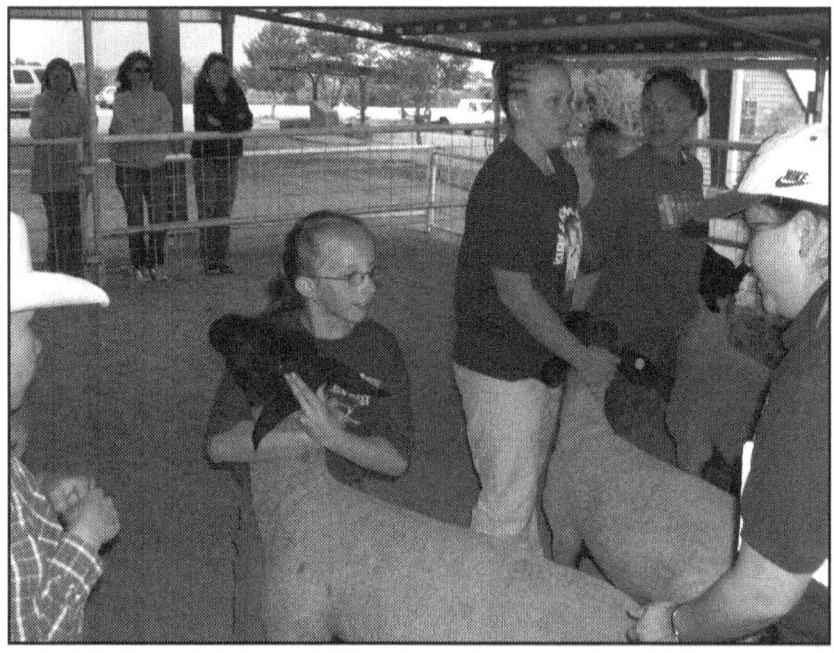

Animals and More—The Santa Fe County Fair offers children and adults a chance to shine.
Photograph courtesy Santa Fe 4-H

A traditional county fair, the Santa Fe version spotlights the work of the youngsters involved in Santa Fe County 4-H as well as produce, livestock and other entries from throughout rural Santa Fe County. Among the highlights in the past have been a frog-jumping contest, a llama show, a herding dog exhibition, horse shows, arts and crafts, home arts and, of course, the livestock auction. The fair also includes children's carnival rides, entertainment and concessions.

INDIAN MARKET
On and around the Plaza
Presented by Southwestern Association for Indian Arts, 983-5220
www.swaia.org
Free

Native Clothing—Santa Fe's annual Indian Market includes a Native American clothing contest. *Photograph courtesy SWAIA*

The third weekend of August brings Santa Fe's biggest event of the year, the annual Indian Market. Held on and around the Plaza the weekend following the third Thursday of the month, this amazing market includes 1200 artists from about 100 tribes who show their work in more than 600 booths. All the work is juried, so you see some of the best examples of a wide-range of Native American talent here.

Buyers, collectors and the curious come to Indian Market to purchase beautiful things, meet the artists and learn about contemporary Indian arts. Dancing, food sales (including favorites such as mutton stew and fry bread with honey or powdered sugar) and demonstrations of various craft techniques add to the market's attraction. A youth market occupies nearby Cathedral Park and Native American children also sell in their parents' booths during Indian Market. SWAIA sponsors Youth Fellowships for Native American artists, age 17 and under, to support their education and artistic development. The cash grant assists with supplies and/or educational opportunities.

The Southwestern Association for Indian Arts Inc. has presented Indian Market since 1922. It is the largest contemporary American Indian art event in the world. To make the market less overwhelming, SWAIA publishes a guide that lists every artist by name and category and includes a map of booth locations. Since the market draws about 80,000 visitors, expect crowds and, kids, keep a close eye on your parents.

SEPTEMBER

FIESTA DE SANTA FE
Zozobra at Fort Marcy Park, 490 Washington Ave.,
Other events on the Plaza and at other locations, 988-7575
www.santafefiesta.org and www.zozobra.com
Most events free

Pets on Parade—The pet parade is one of the best things about the Santa Fe Fiesta.
Photograph by Don Strel

Fiesta is the Spanish word for party, and the Santa Fe Fiesta is a party on the Plaza that mixes tradition and history with music, dancing and food booths. Parades and a pageant are part of the fun, which gets rolling big time beginning on Thursday of the week after Labor Day. Santa Fe's Fiesta proudly calls itself the oldest continuous community celebration in the United States.

Although the Santa Fe Fiesta Council, the non-profit organization which puts on Fiesta, stages concerts long before Fiesta weekend and there are earlier religious events, the Fiesta begins for most people with the burning of *Zozobra*, a giant puppet built to represent all the bad things of the year. Santa Fe artist Will Shuster created *Zozobra*, complete with googly eyes and a ghostly white gown, to personify the disappointments and mistakes of the year. His nickname is Old Man Gloom. Crews of volunteers from the Kiwanis Club build *Zozobra* the week before Fiesta and erect the giant puppet on a huge pole at Fort Marcy Park, 490 Washington Ave., just a few blocks from the Plaza. As the sky grows dark, the puppet comes to life, moaning, growling and waving his hands. (Very young children may be scared.) Finally, after a performance by the Fire Dancers and children dressed as Little Glooms, *Zozobra* disappears in flames to a rowdy chorus of cheers. You'll pay an admission fee (kids get in free) to watch from the field, which is usually VERY crowded.

On Friday comes the *Entrada*, a pageant with the text spoken in Spanish which briefly re-enacts the legendary story of the peaceful return of the Spanish to Santa Fe. Men wearing costumes, members of the *Caballeros deVargas*, take the roles of Captain de Vargas and his men. The Plaza is specially decorated for the *Entrada*, and the rest of Fiesta, with coats of arms of the city's founding families displayed in front of the Palace of the Governors.

Saturday, children and animals have their own parade, one of Fiesta's most charming events. It is called *Defile de Los Ninos*, but commonly known as the pet parade because of the array of animals. Children, parents and pets ranging from cats and dogs to imaginary animals walk in the parade. Many of the animals are also dressed up. Watch from the shade of the Plaza or in front of the Palace of the Governors, just across from the Plaza bandstand. Come early for a good spot. Watching and participating are both free. You usually can sign up to be in the parade at Cathedral Park on Saturday morning before the parade begins.

On Sunday, don't miss Fiesta's biggest parade, the Historical-Hysterical Parade featuring bands, floats of many kinds, clowns, old cars and horses. Like the Pet Parade, the Historical-Hysterical circles the Plaza. The Sunday parade usually assembles in the DeVargas Center parking lot along Paseo de Peralta and makes its way along downtown streets. (The routes for both parades are usually printed in the daily papers.) Fiesta ends Sunday evening with a mass of thanksgiving at the Cathedral Basilica and a candlelight procession to the Cross of the Martyrs.

Throughout Fiesta weekend, the Plaza is alive with free entertainment provided by a variety of local and area music and dance groups, including some composed only of children. Please check the local newspapers for auxiliary carnivals and other family-friendly events. Preceding Fiesta, watch for mariachi concerts and programs by student mariachi groups.

OCTOBER

SUN MOUNTAIN GATHERING:
A New Mexico Native Heritage Festival
Museum Hill, 704-706 Camino Lejo
(Off Old Santa Fe Trail), 476-1250
www.miaclab.org/sunmountain
Free

Living Archaeology—A visitor tries her hand at silver work at the annual Sun Mountain Gathering. *Photo courtesy Museum of Indian Arts & Culture Education Division*

The Museum of Indian Arts & Culture/Laboratory of Anthropology present the annual Sun Mountain Gathering as a way to celebrate 12,000 years of New Mexico's rich cultural heritage.

The weekend event, usually held in early to mid October, includes ancient craft demonstrations, Indian games, archaeology talks and exhibits, Native arts and crafts, Indian music and dancing. Artists and archaeologists demonstrate skills ancient people needed to survive including flint-knapping, arrow making, spear throwing, pottery making, bone tool making, stone axe use, hot rock cooking and heirloom gardening. Hands-on activities for visitors of all ages may include Indian games, tool making, shell bead working, rope making, a chance to use a pump drill and spear throwing lessons and contests.

As part of the event, many Native artists demonstrate their creativity in jewelry, textiles and basketry. Traditional and powwow style dancing, storytelling, drumming and Native music add to the festival. It all happens on and around Milner Plaza, the centerpiece of the Camino Lejo Museum complex.

Members of the World Atlatl Association (WAA) attend to demonstrate the atlatl, an ancient tool for throwing a spear or dart, and instruct people on how to use it. Atlatls and darts are available for those who do not have their own and would like to enter the free competition. Children are welcome to learn and the top winners are presented awards each day.

ALL CHILDREN'S POWWOW
Wheelwright Museum of the American Indian
704 Camino Lejo, 982-4636 or 800-607-4636
www.wheelwright.org
Free

Dance Competition—Native American children dance at the All Children's Powwow.
Photograph by Jane Colman courtesy Wheelwright Museum of the American Indian

The oldest children's powwow in the country, this event attracts more than a hundred young American Indians who perform intertribal, blanket and social dances on either the first or second Saturday of October. Prizes go to the winners in different age groups, and spectators are welcome to take pictures of this colorful event. The powwow usually begins around at 11 a.m. and runs until dusk. If you can't stay the whole time, the Grand Entry that opens the powwow is especially impressive and photogenic. An all-volunteer staff does the organizing. You'll also find American Indian crafts and food sales.

DECEMBER

SANTA FE AT CHRISTMAS

Various events downtown, Canyon Road and at the Indian Pueblos around Santa Fe.
www.museumofnewmexico.org/calendar.cgi
www.indianpueblo.org/index.cfm?module=ipcc&pn=17#dec
www.lensic.com/events.html
www.skisantafe.com

Winter Celebration—Winter sparkles here as Santa Fe decorates the Plaza and the rest of town for the season. *Photograph by Don Strel*

Christmas is one of the best times to be in Santa Fe. On the night before Christmas, the city sparkles. The trees on the Plaza are filled with lights and the Palace of the Governor's Portal—the place where the Indians sit to sell their arts and crafts (See our Places to Visit chapter) is trimmed with pine swags. You'll also see decorations that may be new to you if you aren't from Santa Fe. The little brown lights are called *farolitos* and the bonfires are *luminarias.* You'll see farolitos all over Santa Fe, especially in the older parts of town. They are paper sacks with a few inches of dry sand and a candle inside. When the candle is lit, traditionally on Christmas Eve to guide the way for the Christ Child, it gives out a soft, warm glow. You'll see electric *farolitos*, too, with plastic sacks and a small light bulb instead of a candle. *Farolitos* are placed along roof tops, sidewalks and walls.

Luminarias are less common. You may see them outside of churches before midnight mass both in town and at the nearby Indian Pueblos. You'll also find them on street corners in the Canyon Road area on the night before Christmas. The custom of the fires comes from the story of the shepherds at Bethlehem on the first Christmas. They were told of Jesus' birth by angels while they were standing near a little fire. Another story is that the fires help light the way for Santa.

On Christmas Eve, the city closes Canyon Road to vehicles. Neighborhood residents and shop owners line the sidewalks with *farolitos* and stack the wood high for bonfires. The decorations draw crowds of people into the streets, no matter what the weather. Groups of carolers may stand beside the luminarias, warming themselves while they sing. The Canyon Road *farolito* celebration begins at dusk and continues throughout the evening.

The weeks before Christmas in Santa Fe are filled with concerts and other family events. Among the most unique is *Las Posadas*, an ancient pageant re-enacting Mary and Joseph's search for an inn, presented in Spanish downtown on the Plaza. The procession ends with carols, cookies and hot cider at the Palace of the Governor's courtyard. Christmas at the Palace, a celebration which fills the Palace of the Governors (105 W. Palace Ave) with music, stories and special exhibits, is highly recommended for children and their grownups..

Directly across the street from the Palace, the Museum of Fine Arts (107 W. Palace Ave.) features a holiday open house with a puppet show presenting the historic Gustave Baumann Marionettes. Bauman was a well-known Santa Fe artist, and the event has become a tradition with storytelling, picture taking with a marionette Santa Claus, hot cider and cookies.

The Museum of Indian Arts and Culture (710 Camino Lejo) celebrates the season with its Winterfeast, an afternoon featuring Native American traditional foods drawn from different regions of the Southwest and hands-on educational projects. Please check with the museums for exact dates and times of their events.

On Christmas Eve and Christmas Day, Indian dances at nearby pueblos are open to the public. Among the places you can watch the dances are Picuris, San Juan, Taos, Acoma, Laguna, San Felipe, Santa Ana, Tesuque and San Ildefonso Pueblos. And speaking of dance, in Santa Fe you might also find a holiday performance of The Nutcracker featuring children as well as adult dancers.

The Santa Fe Ski Area, located 16 miles northeast and 3,000 feet above the Santa Fe Plaza, usually opens on Thanksgiving Day, so skiing can be part of the holiday tradition.

YEAR-ROUND

FREE COMMUNITY CONCERTS
Santa Fe Concert Band, various venues, 986-9073
www.santafeconcertband.org

Founded in 1869, this volunteer band is devoted to continuing one of Santa Fe's oldest traditions, free public concerts indoor and out presenting accessible music played by volunteer musicians.

This tradition dates back more than 120 years, when Francisco Pérez, after serving as a Confederate Army bugler in the ill-fated invasion of New Mexico by Texas forces during the Civil War, returned to Santa Fe and formed *La Banda de Santa Fe*. The band continued under various names and directors. From 1909 through 1940, the band was called Los Conquistadores. The Santa Fe Concert Band was formally incorporated in 1983.

The schedule normally includes outdoor concerts for Mother's Day, Memorial Day, Father's Day, the Fourth of July, a mid and late summer concert, a Fiesta concert and a Christmas concert. The outdoor concerts begin at 2 p.m. and are usually held on the Plaza or at Federal Park (Paseo Peralta at Washington Avenue). The informal settings make the music especially accessible for children. This is a great way to introduce your child to "serious" music.

STORY HOURS

Borders Books, Music and Café
500 Montezuma Avenue, 954-4707

Collected Works Bookstore
208-B W. San Francisco, 988-4226
www.collectedworksbookstore.com

Santa Fe Public Library
La Farge,1730 Llano Street, 955-4860
Main, 145 Washington Avenue, 955-6783
Bookstop, Villa Linda Center, 4250 Cerrillos Road, 955-2980
santafelibrary.org

Wheelwright Museum of the American Indian
704 Camino Lejo, 982-4636.
www.wheelwright.org

Vista Grande Public Library
14 Avenida Torreon, Eldorado, 466-7323
Free

An hour with a good story, whether read from a book or improvised face-to-face, introduces children to a world where imagination reigns supreme. Santa Fe offers a variety of possibilities, beginning with those listed above. In addition, *New Mexico Kids!* and *Tumbleweeds*, two family-friendly newspapers, can tell you what's happening. Santa Fe's daily newspapers also list story telling sessions and other events for children in their calendars.

At the Wheelwright, a gem of a museum, you'll find free story telling and related art projects once a month on Saturday. During the summer, parents and children enjoy the well-told tall tales and traditional New Mexican stories from professional story teller and author Joe Hayes. These stories are told outdoors—bring a blanket, pillow or lawn chair to sit on.

Borders and Collected Works book stores have regular free story times as do the children's rooms at the libraries. The libraries usually offer programs for pre-schoolers throughout the year and summer programs for school age children. School classes and home-schooled children are invited to visit the library for tours, instruction and, of course, books to take home.

ALBUQUERQUE

SUMMER

FAMILY FESTIVALS
National Hispanic Cultural Center
1701 4th Street SW, Albuquerque, 246-2261
www.nhccnm.org
Children 16 and younger admitted free.

SUMMERFEST
Civic Plaza, 400 Marquette NW, 768-3556
www.cabq.gov/crs/specialevents.html
Free

SUMMER MUSIC FOR FAMILIES
Rio Grande Zoo, 903 10th Street SW
Rio Grande Botanic Garden, 2601 Central Ave. NW
764-6200 info for both
www.cabq.gov/biopark/common/summernights.html
www.cabq.gov/biopark/zoo/educationzoomusic.html

New Mexico's biggest city offers several summer events of interest to families. Among them are free music and activities at Civic Plaza, and concerts at the zoo and botanic garden.

In June and July, Albuquerque invites everyone to come downtown for free outdoor concerts and mini-festivals, events known as Summerfest. Staged at Civic Plaza for many years, Summerfest has highlighted different cultures with food, games, dance, costumes and music as part of the fun.

From June through August, the Albuquerque Biological Park welcomes visitors to Summer Nights programs in the beautiful and peaceful setting of the Botanic Garden. Traditionally held on Thursday evenings in June, July and August, the series features live musical entertainment. The performers, local and regional talent, vary from week to week as does the style of music. In addition to country, folk, bluegrass, Caribbean and Cajun tunes, visitors are entertained by a magic show, a caricature artist and model boats on the pond. There is a reduced admission fee for children. Seating is on the lawn and you're welcome to bring along blankets and folding chairs.

Zoo Music—The Rio Grande Zoo hosts family concerts in Albuquerque in the summer.
Photo by Terry Axline courtesy of the Albuquerque Biological Park.

For more than a decade, the Rio Grande Zoo has enticed visitors from June through mid-August with the Zoo Music Concert Series. Zoo Music is a popular, lively event where families can enjoy an evening of entertainment in a unique setting. The music includes Cajun, zydeco, bluegrass, Celtic, rock, jazz and more. Local, regional, national and even international talent performs under the band shell most Friday evenings in the summer. Children's tickets are sold at a reduced price, and visitors have a chance to see the animals after normal zoo hours. Because it's lawn seating only, bring blankets or your own folding chairs.

The National Hispanic Cultural Center hosts Family Days/Community Days in the spring and fall. The festivals include outdoor entertainment, art and craft activities, storytellers and food booths. Sometimes the center gives away books and school supplies. The festivals are often in conjunction with *Día del Niño/Cinco de Mayo*, a special honoring of children, which takes place the last weekend in April, and *Día de los Muertos*, or the Day of Dead, at the end of October/beginning of November.

SEPTEMBER

NEW MEXICO STATE FAIR
State Fair Grounds, 300 San Pedro Blvd. N.E, Albuquerque
265-1791
exponm.com/cms/index.php?fair
Children receive discounted admission

The New Mexico State Fair is one of the state's most popular events. In fact, the fair's attendance records usually top all but two other shows in the West (the Texas State Fair and the Houston Livestock Show and Rodeo).

The State Fair runs for 18 days beginning in early September. You'll find free schedules of each day's events and a map of the grounds at the information booth as you enter. The fair's attractions include 16 nights of rodeo with a day of bull-riding competitions and accompanying concerts with big-name country stars in Tingley Coliseum. The fair also offers daily horse shows and competitions for the best in many categories of animals, produce and hand-made items. Animal exhibits include a large petting farm and demonstrations of milking machines with patient cows. At the Creative and Home Arts exhibits, you'll find everything from dolls to homemade doughnuts. And don't miss the art gallery.

The Kid's Park Midway for ages 12 and younger features its own rides and two stages for performances, which include magic shows and puppet theater. The larger midway has rides to thrill older visitors and even their parents!

Food at the fair encompasses an amazing variety, from turkey legs to ice cream, served by more than 100 vendors in virtually every corner of the fair grounds. Don't overlook Indian Village, *Villa Hispana* and Pioneer Village, all of which serve their own special dishes along with a menu of pleasing entertainment. All of the exhibits at the fair and much of the entertainment are included in the price of admission. (The rodeo and the midway are the main exceptions.)

Located on the 236-acre Expo New Mexico grounds in the heart of Albuquerque, the fair was established long before New Mexico became a state. In 1881, the New Mexico Agricultural, Mineral and Industrial Exposition, the grandmother of today's state fair, opened its doors and ran for five days. Despite relentless rain, the initial exposition was highly popular with both residents and business owners. The fair was born!

Early territorial fairs featured parachute jumps from hot-air balloons, lawn tennis tournaments, Indian races, Vaudeville-style shows and trapeze artists. These fairs also recognized New Mexico's strong Native American and Hispanic influences exhibited in artwork, cuisine, and traditional dances and ceremonies, themes that have continued to the modern version of the fair.

SEPTEMBER-OCTOBER

ALBUQUERQUE INTERNATIONAL BALLOON FIESTA
Balloon Fiesta Park, between Alameda and Tramway N.E.,
west of I-25, Albuquerque 821-1000 or (888) 422-7277
www.aibf.org
Children 12 and under free

Big Fun—The Albuquerque Balloon Fiesta offers colorful fun. *Courtesy Albuquerque International Balloon Fiesta*

If you live anywhere in New Mexico or are planning a visit in the fall, don't miss this event! It's the largest balloon festival in the world.

Held for 10 days over two weekends each year in late September and early October, the Balloon Fiesta draws hundreds of balloons and pilots to New Mexico. Beginning with the first gathering of 13 balloons in 1972, the event caught on. By 1978 Albuquerque was host to the world's most popular ballooning event, and it kept getting bigger and better.

Huge colorful hot air balloons are the main attraction. The balloon fiesta highlights the balloons with a variety of events which give spectators an up-close view. Events such as mass ascensions, balloon glows and special shape rodeos draw pilots from more than 28 different countries and visitors from around the world. If you plan to come, don't wait too long to make a room reservation in Santa Fe or Albuquerque!

The fiesta's most popular events are the mass ascensions, when hundreds of balloons are in the air at once, and the balloon glows which feature tethered balloon lit from the inside. The mass ascension, an early morning launch of all the participating balloons, has been a feature of Balloon Fiesta since its earliest days. Weather permitting, balloons begin to launch at about 7:15 a.m., led by a balloon flying the American flag to the strains of "The Star Spangled Banner." The balloon glows were invented in Albuquerque in 1979, when local pilots inflated balloons on Christmas Eve night as a thank you to local residents. "Glow" events are now held all over the world. Balloon Glows are crowd pleasers, in part because you don't have to get up early to see the show! The mass ascension and the balloon glows (which are followed by fireworks displays) are great opportunities for photographs.

One of the best things about the Balloon Fiesta is that visitors have a chance to watch as the balloons are unloaded and inflated, and see the moment the balloon basket leaves the ground. The fiesta uses volunteers to help the pilots; call or check the website for more information.

If you'd like to try a balloon ride yourself, commercial pilots offer you that chance during the event. Food, beverages and balloon-related merchandise are for sale on the Fiesta grounds. To reduce traffic to the fair grounds, combination tickets that include a bus ride from a central parking area and admission are available.

RECOMMENDED READING:

Here are a few books about Santa Fe, New Mexico or aspects of life in the Southwest that I enjoy. If you'd like to recommend a title, please contact me at Sunstone Press.

Anaya, Rudolfo. *My Land Sings, Stories from the Rio Grande.* Harper Trophy, 1999
_____. *The Santero's Miracle, A Bilingual Story.* University of New Mexico Press, 2004

Berry, Michael. *Georgia O'Keeffe Painter, American Women of Achievement Series.* Chelsea House Publishing, 1991

Bullock, Alice. *Living Legends of the Santa Fe Country.* Sunstone Press, 1985
_____. *Loretto and the Miraculous Staircase.* Sunstone Press, 1978
_____. *Mountain Villages.* Sunstone Press, 1981
_____. *Monumental Ghosts.* Sunstone Press, 1987

Carson, William C. *Peter Becomes a Trail Man.* University of New Mexico Press, 2002

Chapman, Al. *Santos of Spanish New Mexico, A Coloring Book.* Sunstone Press, 1982

Chavez, Fray Angelico. *La Conquistadora.* Sunstone Press, 1983

de Paola, Tomie. *The Night of Las Posadas.* Putnam, 1999

Ebinger, Virginia Nylander. *Niñez, Spanish Songs, Games and Stories of Childhood*, Sunstone Press, 1993

Eggers, Bob. *Santa Fe After Dark.* Sunstone Press, 2004
Grossman, Virginia and Long, Sylvia. *Ten Little Rabbits.* Chronicle Books, 1991

Hayes, Joe. *The Day it Snowed Tortillas: Tales for Spanish New Mexico.* Mariposa Books, 1982 (and other books by Joe Hayes)

Hillerman, Anne. *Done in the Sun.* Sunstone Press, 1983

Hillerman, Tony. *The Boy Who Made Dragonfly.* University of New Mexico Press, 1972.

Hobbs, Will. *Kokopelli's Flute.* Avon Camelot Books, 1997

Hodge, Gene Meany. *Kachina Tales from the Indian Pueblos.* Sunstone Press, 1993

Hyde, Hazel. *Maria Making Pottery.* Sunstone Press, 1973

Kreischer, Elsie Karr. *Maria Montoya Martinez Master Potter.* Publican Publishing Company, 1995

Krenz, Nancy, and Byrnes, Patricia. *Southwestern Arts and Crafts Projects.* Sunstone Press, 1979

Martinez, Eluid Levi. *What is a New Mexico Santo?* Sunstone Press, 1978

McCord, Richard. *The Other State New Mexico, USA.* Sunstone Press, 2003

Mora, Pat. Maria Paints the Hills. Museum of New Mexico Press, 2002
　　　　　. The Desert is My Mother El Desierto es Mi Madre. Pinata Books. 1994
　　　　　. The Song of Francis and the Animals, Eerdmans Books, 2005

Morand, Sheila. *Santa Fe Then and Now.* Sunstone Press, 1998

Murphy, Barbara Beasley. *Life I Love You.* Museum of New Mexico Press, 2004
　　　　　　　　　　　. *Miguel Lost and Found at the Palace.* Museum of New Mexico Press, 2002

Ortega, Pedro Ribera. *Christmas in Old Santa Fe.* Sunstone Press, 1973

Owings, Jennifer Dewey. *Paisano the Roadrunner.* Millbrook Press, Inc., 2002
　　　　　　　　and Fleming, Jeanie Puleson. *Zozobra, The Story of Old Man Gloom.* University of New Mexico Press, 2004

Raciti, James J. *Old Santa Fe.* Sunstone Press, 2003

Reed, Evelyn. *Coyote Tales from the Indian Pueblos.* Sunstone Press, 1988

Russell, Marion adapted by Ginger Wadsworth. *Along the Santa Fe Trail.* Albert Whitman and Company, 1993

Silverman, Jason. *Untold New Mexico*. Sunstone Press 2005

Simmons, Marc. *Yesterday in Santa Fe*. Sunstone Press, 1989
_____. *New Mexico Mavericks*. Sunstone Press, 2005

Smith, Marylou M. *My Grandmother's Adobe Dollhouse*. New Mexico Magazine Press, Route 66 Publishing, 1984.

Talbert, Marc. *A Sunburned Prayer*. Aladin Paperbacks, 1995

Tripp, Valerie. *Meet Josefina, An American Girl*. Pleasant Co. Publishers, 1997 (and other books in the Josefina series)

Winter, Jeanette. *My Name is Georgia*. Harcourt Brace, 1998

Wood, Nancy. *Old Coyote*. Candlewick Press, 2004

Woodword, John. *The Secret World of Prairie Dogs*. Raintree Press, 2004

Yoder, Walter. *The Big New Mexico Activity Book*. Sunstone Press, 1993

www.ingramcontent.com/pod-product-compliance
Lightning Source LLC
Chambersburg PA
CBHW022100160426

43198CB00008B/302